Lad Culture in Higher Education

Responding to increasing concerns about the harmful effects of so-called 'lad culture' in British universities, and related 'bro' and 'frat' cultures in US colleges, this book is the first to explore and analyse the perspectives of university staff on these cultures, which students suggest foster the normalisation of sexism, homophobia, racism, sexual harassment and violence.

Drawing on in-depth interviews with a broad range of staff and faculty across different types of universities in England, the book explores the following key questions:

- What is lad culture?
- How and where is it manifest in higher education and what are the effects on students and staff?
- How can 'laddish' behaviour be explained?
- How can we theorise lad culture to enable us to better understand and challenge it?
- How do dynamics in the United Kingdom compare to so-called 'bro' and 'frat' cultures in US colleges?

By examining the ways in which lad culture is understood and explained, the authors illustrate that current understandings of lad culture obscure the broader processes through which problematic attitudes, practices, and educational climates are fostered. This analysis enables a theorisation of lad culture that makes visible the gendered norms and intersecting structural inequalities that underpin it.

This timely and accessible volume will be of great interest to anyone looking to understand and tackle sexism, sexual harassment and violence in and beyond university contexts. It will be of particular significance to researchers, undergraduate and postgraduate students, academics, and policy makers in the fields of gender and sexuality in education, higher education, and sociology of education.

Carolyn Jackson is Professor of Gender and Education at Lancaster University, UK.

Vanita Sundaram is Professor of Education at the University of York, UK.

Routledge Critical Studies in Gender and Sexuality in Education

Series Editors Wayne Martino, Emma Renold, Goli Rezai-Rashti, Jessica Ringrose and Nelson Rodriguez

13 **Learning to Live in Boys' Schools**
   Art-Led Understandings of Masculinities
   Donal O'Donoghue

14 **Starting with Gender in International Higher Education Research**
   Conceptual Debates and Methodological Considerations
   Edited by Emily F. Henderson and Z Nicolazzo

15 **Women, Islam, and Education in Iran**
   Edited by Goli M. Rezai-Rashti, Golnar Mehran, and Shirin Abdmolaei

16 **Gender and Care in Teaching Young Children**
   A Material Feminist Approach to Early Childhood Education
   Denise Hodgins

17 **Gender, Definitional Politics and 'Live' Knowledge Production**
   Contesting Concepts at Conferences
   Emily F. Henderson

18 **Girls, Single-sex Schools, and Postfeminist Fantasies**
   Stephanie D. McCall

19 **Latina Students' Experiences in Public Schools**
   Educational Equity and Gender
   Susan McCullough

20 **Lad Culture in Higher Education**
   Sexism, Sexual Harassment and Violence
   Carolyn Jackson and Vanita Sundaram

For more information about this series, please visit: https://www.routledge.com

Lad Culture in Higher Education

Sexism, Sexual Harassment and Violence

Carolyn Jackson and Vanita Sundaram

NEW YORK AND LONDON

First published 2020
by Routledge
52 Vanderbilt Avenue, New York, NY 10017

and by Routledge
2 Park Square, Milton Park, Abingdon, Oxon, OX14 4RN

Routledge is an imprint of the Taylor & Francis Group, an informa business

© 2020 Taylor & Francis

The right of Carolyn Jackson and Vanita Sundaram to be identified as authors of this work has been asserted by them in accordance with sections 77 and 78 of the Copyright, Designs and Patents Act 1988.

All rights reserved. No part of this book may be reprinted or reproduced or utilised in any form or by any electronic, mechanical, or other means, now known or hereafter invented, including photocopying and recording, or in any information storage or retrieval system, without permission in writing from the publishers.

Trademark notice: Product or corporate names may be trademarks or registered trademarks, and are used only for identification and explanation without intent to infringe.

Library of Congress Cataloging-in-Publication Data
A catalog record for this title has been requested

ISBN: 9781138571310 (hbk)
ISBN: 9780203702901 (ebk)

Typeset in Sabon
by codeMantra

Printed and bound in Great Britain by
TJ International Ltd, Padstow, Cornwall

Carolyn dedicates the book to Steve Dempster (1970–2017), a valued colleague, friend and scholar.

Vanita dedicates the book to Kamala, her mother and first feminist teacher.

Contents

	Acknowledgements	ix
	Introduction	1
1	'Show Us Your Tits and We'll Buy you Shots': Lad Culture, Sexual Harassment and Violence in Higher Education	14
2	'But Most of It's Banter': What Does Lad Culture Look like in Higher Education in England?	33
3	'They're Mainly Private School, White Boys': Who Are the Lads?	61
4	'But They're Not Really like That': Explanations for Laddism	86
5	(Re)theorising and Addressing Lad Culture	109
	Conclusion	131
	Appendix	137
	References	139
	Index	149

Acknowledgements

Lots of people have supported our research project and book. We are both very grateful to the Society for Research into Higher Education (SRHE) for funding this research and to Louise Morley who was an advisor for the research project. We are indebted to the interviewees who gave their time and support so generously, and in some cases also facilitated access to their institutions. Thanks are due to Dee Daglish who provided administrative support, Maggie Lackey who transcribed all of the interviews, Rebecca Marsden who constructed and supported the project website, and Annis Stead who undertook data coding. We are also extremely grateful to our network of feminist colleagues and friends who offer ongoing support and help us to develop our ideas and work. Specific thanks are due to colleagues who read and provided helpful feedback on chapters: Chris Marlow, Alison Phipps, and Jo Warin. Special thanks go to Wayne Martino who encouraged and supported this book throughout. In sections of the book we have drawn upon our article – '"I have a sense that it's probably quite bad ... but because I don't see it, I don't know": staff perspectives on "lad culture" in higher education' – which was previously published (2018) in the journal *Gender and Education*; we are grateful to Taylor and Francis for permission to do this (https://www.tandfonline.com). We also have some personal acknowledgements.

Carolyn's – There are lots of references in this book to the work of Steve Dempster who was one of the first scholars to undertake research on lad culture in higher education. I had the pleasure of supervising Steve's PhD (with Jo Warin) and subsequently he became a very valued colleague and friend. Steve died in 2017 at the age of 46. I miss him tremendously. I have lost count of the number of times while writing this volume that I wanted to talk to him about lad culture. I am pleased, though, that our use of his written work means he is part of this book. I have dedicated the book to Steve.

I would like to thank colleagues/friends in Educational Research at Lancaster University for their ongoing care and support, as well as friends outside academia. Jan Lees and Paula Shakespeare deserve special thanks – they are such generous friends who are always there, often

x *Acknowledgements*

with food, help, and even furniture! My mum and dad – Brenda and John Jackson – remain a constant source of love, support, and encouragement. I cannot thank them enough.

Part way through the project I fell in love with Heike Horsburgh. Heike enhances and enriches my life in countless ways, every day. She is an inspirational woman and I have learned so much from her. Words cannot convey my love and gratitude.

Vanita's – The process of writing this book has been revelatory for me in a number of ways. The entrenched misogyny, classism, and racism of higher education institutions have been starkly revealed through our fieldwork, through our analysis of our participants' experiences, and of institutional practices and policies. Much has been revealed about the intersectional nature of sexualised violence in higher education and the need to consider how homophobia and transphobia are layered upon racism, classism, hetero-sexism, and other forms of marginalisation and oppression. I am so grateful to our participants for sharing what were sometimes painful experiences, for being honest about their personal and professional navigations through institutional processes, and for talking openly with us about gaps and failings in these.

Personally, the process of writing this book has revealed to me the power of community, the importance of friendship, and how lucky I am to be working within an incredible community of feminist scholars, so many of whom I consider close friends. A prolonged period of ill health during the writing of this book revealed the strength of these friendships, which sustained me, gave me hope, nurtured me, and reassured me during a time of uncertainty, fear, and self-doubt. In particular, I would like to express my gratitude to Deb Ollis, Alison Phipps, Tiffany Page, and Jessica Ringrose. This book would not have been completed without the drive, vision, and labour of Carolyn Jackson. She is generous, caring, thoughtful, and has been a huge source of support during my illness, during this project, and in the many years leading up to it. She is an incredible mentor, from whom I have learned so much about the practice of feminist ethics and research. Thank you, CJ.

I lost my mother during the period in which we were writing this book. She was a pioneer of her generation: moving across continents to marry my father and, eventually, to have her two children; learning to speak a fourth language (a notoriously difficult one to master at that!); re-training and carving out a successful career; learning and adopting new customs and norms; and passing these on to her daughters. Through her own life experiences, she taught us to be outraged; she taught us not to accept the status quo; she taught us that we needed to play a part in dismantling systems and structures of inequality. She was my first feminist teacher, and I would not be the woman I am – or the academic I ended up being – without her. I hope to be half as courageous, determined, and fierce as she was.

Introduction

> The National Union of Students (NUS) has said it is happy to see the Government take the issue of lad culture seriously after Business Secretary Sajid Javid ordered an inquiry into sexist behaviour at British universities ... Mr Javid this week asked Universities UK to set up and lead a taskforce in order to develop a code of practice to bring about cultural change.
>
> (*The Independent*, 8/9/15)

Concerns about lad culture[1] in UK universities have mushroomed over the last seven years or so. Driven initially by the National Union of Students (NUS),[2] worries are now voiced across the higher education sector and were sufficient to prompt the Conservative Government to order an inquiry in 2015, as signalled in the opening quotation from *The Independent* (8/9/15). Concerns have also been writ large in the media: reports about lad culture emerged in the UK press around late 2012 and there has been coverage in all major newspapers. In what Phipps and Young (2015a, 306) refer to as a 'minor media storm', headlines have included: 'Sexist Lads' Culture is out of control at Universities' (*Daily Mail*, 16/9/14); 'Lad culture: What can be done when it's everywhere at university?' (*Independent.co.uk*, 6/1/15); 'Ingrained sexism and lad banter: Why rape culture is still alive at British Universities' (*The Daily Telegraph*, 7/1/16); and '#MeToo on campus: UK universities investigate sexual assaults themselves – As more women speak up over sexual violence, universities are cracking down on "lad culture"' (*The Guardian*, 31/7/18). Early accounts of lad culture in the press tended to be based on anecdotal accounts of practices such as 'slut dropping' (where male students offer women lifts home after night-time socials but leave them stranded miles away from home) and 'hazing' (initiation ceremonies usually linked to male sports teams), as well as fancy dress parties with themes such as 'pimps and hoes' and 'geeks and sluts' (*The Independent*, 11/10/2012). Reports continued, and cases identified as reflecting lad culture included the production and circulation by the men's rugby club at the London School of Economics of leaflets which had sexist

2 *Introduction*

and homophobic content (*The Guardian*, 06/10/2014), and students at Nottingham University singing a misogynistic chant that included a line about digging up a female corpse and having sex with it (*Daily Mirror*, 25/10/2014).

Although there have been increasingly widespread concerns voiced about lad culture in universities, how lad culture is perceived and understood in higher education contexts remains unclear: this is the focus of our book. To explore understandings of lad culture in university contexts we draw in particular on data generated during our interviews with a wide range of staff across six English universities. Our focus on staff perspectives is both novel and important. Our research is the first to explore staff perspectives in the United Kingdom and thus extends and complements previous work exploring students' views. We address the following key questions: What is lad culture? How and where is it manifest in higher education? Who is laddish? How is laddish behaviour explained?[3] How can we (re)theorise lad culture? What are the implications for higher education institutions? In exploring these questions we engage with discourses[4] about lad culture within and outside educational contexts, and academic research on lad culture, sexual harassment, and violence in higher education in the United Kingdom and internationally. As such, below we introduce discourses about lad culture in society generally, before turning our focus to educational contexts: compulsory education and then higher education.

Lad Culture in UK Society

The discourse of laddism, or 'new' laddism, gained renewed prominence in the United Kingdom in the 1990s (Dempster, 2007; Phipps, 2017a). Discourses about lads were evident in the 1970s, but, as we discuss in the next section, these were strongly associated with white working-class boys' resistance to middle-class school cultures, largely because of the work of Paul Willis (1977). We also highlight in the next section how associations between laddism and working-class boys regained renewed traction in the 1990s in light of worries about boys' 'underachievement' in school. However, at the same time discourses about laddism (or new laddism) in society more broadly were becoming increasingly dominant, and, although maintaining some associations with working-class masculinities, they extended across social class groups (Francis, 1999; Dempster, 2007; Phipps, 2017a). Phipps (2017a) and others suggest that this more middle-class version of laddism was exemplified by so-called lads' mags such as *Loaded* and the TV sitcom *Men Behaving Badly*. Research suggests that Lads' mags in the United Kingdom (and United States) are characterised by themes and images of women as sexual objects, stereotypical sexual roles, privileging of heteronormative male sex drive discourses, and widespread sexist attitudes (Romero-Sanchez et al., 2017). They also show women as 'sexual prey for men to conquer and consume' (Romero-Sanchez et al., 2017, 518).

Such was the dominance of (new) laddism in the 1990s that Rosalind Gill, writing in 2003, argued that over the previous decade there had been two dominant, enduring constructions of masculinity: the 'new lad' and the 'new man'. According to Gill (2003, 37) the new lad is

> depicted as hedonistic, post- (if not anti) feminist, and pre-eminently concerned with beer, football and "shagging" women ... A key feature of some constructions of "new lad" is the emphasis on his knowing and ironic relationship to the world of serious adult concerns.

The new lad is often presented as a reaction against the new man, with the new man being portrayed as 'sensitive, emotionally aware, respectful of women, and egalitarian in outlook' (Gill, 2003, 37). Furthermore, as the new man is seen to be a product of feminism, the new lad is often regarded as a backlash against feminism (Benyon, 2002). It has been argued then that contemporary laddism 'is primarily an attempt to put women back in their place' (Phipps, 2017a, 824; see also Garcia-Favaro and Gill, 2016).

While laddism is primarily associated with men and masculinities, in the mid-1990s the UK media constructed the 'ladette': the female version of a lad. Ladettes were initially presented as predominantly post-school-age young women, with DJs Sara Cox and Zoe Ball and television presenter Denise Van Outen being very strongly associated with ladette culture. Ladettes were portrayed as hedonistic, into heaving drinking, and as prioritising careers and casual sex over marriage, motherhood, and domesticity (Jackson and Tinkler, 2007). Jackson and Tinkler's (2007) work, which explored media representations of ladettes, suggested that portraits of ladettes were almost invariably critical. Ladettes were critiqued both for attempting to be 'like a man' and at the same time they were derided for failing to meet men's standards. Jackson and Tinkler (2007) illustrate how critiques of ladettes in the press were often couched in terms of concerns about women's health and social order issues. However, their analysis suggests that ladettes were demonised because of their potential to disrupt the gender order, and especially dominant discourses on women as carers. Thus, press-led responses to ladettes were also about putting women back in their place.

Although the press initially presented ladettes as post-school-age, by the 2000s these concerns extended to schoolgirls: 'the "ladette" culture has filtered down from women in their mid-20s to girls who are still at

4 *Introduction*

school' (*The Guardian*, 15/12/2004, 10). It is to concerns about lad culture in schools that we now turn.

Lad Culture in School

Although Conservative Government ministers are now calling upon *universities* to tackle lad culture, in the mid-to-late 1990s and early 2000s there were demands from the then New Labour Government for *secondary schools* to tackle lad culture and laddism. However, the use of the same terms – laddism or lad culture – by Government ministers in relation to these two education sectors belies important differences in the nature and focus of the anxieties in these contexts. In secondary schools, the concerns were focused upon laddish anti-learning and/or anti-school cultures, and were voiced in tandem with anxieties about boys' so-called 'underachievement' (Francis, 1999; Jackson, 2006, 2010). The association between laddism and boys' underachievement was articulated by David Blunkett when he was Secretary of State for Education, and repeated by other education ministers in what became a dominant discourse.

> We face a genuine problem of underachievement among boys, particularly those from working class families. This underachievement is linked to a laddish culture which in many areas has grown out of deprivation, and a lack of both self-confidence and opportunity.
> (Department for Education and Employment, 2000)

> We have to crack the lad culture that stops too many young boys doing well at school ... The culture tells boys that it is fine to play around and not work hard. But this harms their chances of doing well, getting their exams and fulfilling their potential.
> (David Miliband, then School Standards
> Minister, cited by Clare, 2003, 5)

In secondary school contexts laddism was portrayed as a dominant form of masculinity that involved '"having a laugh" ... disruptive behaviour, objectifying women' (Francis, 1999, 357), liking and playing sport (especially football), wearing the 'right' sorts of clothes, 'hanging out' with mates, and a rejection of overt academic hard work' (Jackson, 2010a, 506). Jackson's interviews with secondary school teachers suggested that they perceived laddism in schools to involve: 'group behaviours; attention seeking; competition; (publicly) prioritising sport over academic work; avoidance of overt academic work; disruptive behaviours; and lack of respect for authority' (Jackson, 2010, 509). There are parallels between discourses about laddism in secondary school and university contexts: in both the focus is principally on boys/men and masculinities

Introduction 5

(although see Jackson, 2006a, 2006b) and there are shared characteristics, for example, having a laugh, objectifying women, being sociable, associations with sport. However, there are also important distinctions in terms of focus and degree. In schools, the major concerns were twofold. First, there was significant concern about boys disrupting classrooms and learning – adversely affecting their own learning as well as that of others. Second, core to representations of laddism was the notion that cool lads could not be seen to work hard academically, as overt academic effort was discursively positioned as uncool and therefore to be avoided (Frosh, Phoenix and Pattman, 2001; Younger and Warrington, 2005; Jackson, 2006a; Francis, Skelton and Read, 2012). The association between being a lad and presenting academic effort as uncool is reflected in Miliband's earlier comments. Blunkett's comments emphasise the association between laddism, underachievement, and social class, suggesting that laddism and ergo underachievement are particularly associated with working-class boys. Such an association is likely to have its roots in Paul Willis' (1977) work as flagged earlier, in which he used the term lads to describe a group of white, working-class, anti-school boys. Thus, as Francis (1999) argues, in the 1970s and 1980s the term lads was particularly associated with white, working-class, young men. To some extent that association continued beyond the 1980s, as Blunkett's comments attest. However, as discussed earlier, Francis (1999) and others have demonstrated that the association broadened in the 1990s and the values of lads were appropriated by and popularised for middle-class boys and men.

There has rightly been a lot of critique of the associations delineated in the previous paragraph. First, feminists have been very critical of what has been referred to as a 'moral panic' (Epstein et al., 1998) about boys' 'underachievement'. Most representations of underachieving boys in media, government, and popular discourses were highly problematic as all too often they ignored important questions such as which boys are underachieving? How is underachievement defined – in relation to what or whom, and why? Which girls are also underachieving? (Jackson, 2006a). The association between laddism, underachievement, and social class is also problematic, as research (Jackson, 2006a; Francis, Skelton and Read, 2010, 2012) illustrates that many laddish boys are high achievers, and many laddish boys are middle class. Thus, contrary to depictions in the press, research suggests a complex picture.

The focus on boys' 'underachievement' also led to girls' concerns and experiences being side-lined (Jackson, Paechter and Renold, 2010). Furthermore, while concerns about schoolboys and laddism dominated the agenda, concerns about schoolgirls and laddism were more muted. However, as mentioned in the previous section, they did emerge. Jackson (2006a, 2006b) explored discourses about laddish girls in school through interviews with over 150 pupils and 30 staff across six

6 Introduction

secondary schools in England. She argued that the concerns about girls and boys in relation to laddism were very differently framed by teachers. Jackson (2006b, 355) argues that:

> For boys, concerns about 'laddish' behaviours in school centre largely around raising their academic achievements and reducing disruption in class. For girls, the focus is less explicitly on raising achievement because, according to dominant education discourses, girls are 'successful'. Concerns about 'ladettes' relate to them disrupting classes, but also to their sexuality, safety and morality; femininity remains a 'moral condition' (Smith, 1998, cited in Francis, 2000). For example, some teachers were explicit about finding drinking much more worrying when the drinkers were girls than when they were boys; the same also applied to fighting.

Jackson (2006b) highlights stark gender double-standards where, like the press's treatment of ladettes, girls and women are judged very harshly and relatively more harshly than boys and men. Unfortunately, while teachers were concerned about laddish girls transgressing gender boundaries, they were unconcerned about the aspects of laddism that were the cause of most concern in relation to boys, and potentially could be detrimental to girls' results, as Jackson (2006b, 356) argued:

> Time and time again girls across the schools told me that it is not 'cool' for girls to be seen to work hard on school work … But although concerns about the implications of such attitudes are central to discourses on 'laddishness' and boys' 'underachievement' … they have not been raised in relation to 'ladettes' or other girls … it is worth noting at this point that those who are concerned about 'anti-school, it's-not-cool-to-be-seen-working' attitudes amongst boys, should also be concerned about such attitudes amongst girls.

There are striking parallels in relation to lad culture in higher education. As we explore in Chapter 3, while lad culture in higher education is primarily associated with men, like in schools, laddish women were judged differently and relatively more harshly than their men counterparts, with the same discourses about women's drinking and fighting being evident across school and university contexts.

Overall, whereas the focus on boys' laddism in schools was on academic 'underachievement', the focus in higher education is less on academic issues and contexts and more on social spaces. However, as we demonstrate later, laddism is an issue in academic contexts in some universities (see also Jackson and Dempster, 2009; Jackson et al., 2015). Furthermore, increasingly there is attention in schools to sexual harassment and violence following a Women and Equalities Committee

Inquiry in 2016 (Women and Equalities Committee, 2016). Thus, the agendas relating to lad culture in schools and universities increasingly seem to be converging.

Lad Culture in Higher Education

Although there has been considerable media interest in lad culture in UK higher education contexts, research in this sphere is still in its infancy. This research is discussed in the next chapter, so here we provide only a very brief introduction. The existing research has focused exclusively on students' perspectives about, and experiences of, laddism (Dempster, 2007, 2009; 2011; Warin and Dempster, 2007; NUS, 2013; Jackson, Dempster and Pollard, 2015; Phipps and Young, 2015a, 2015b; Lewis, Marine and Kenny, 2018; Jeffries, 2019; Stentiford, 2019; Diaz-Fernandez and Evans, 2019a). For example, The *Hidden Marks* study (NUS, 2010) utilised a survey to explore women students' experiences of physical intimidation, fear, and verbal, sexualised, and physical harassment and violence, and revealed that two-thirds of respondents reported having experienced some form of verbal or non-verbal harassment in or around their institution. Phipps and Young's (NUS, 2013) qualitative study similarly found that experiences of misogyny – ranging from the objectification of women to physical and sexualised harassment – were prevalent for women university students in their sample. Their work drew explicitly on the concept of lad culture in higher education, characterising it as 'a group or "pack" mentality residing in activities such as sport and heavy alcohol consumption, and "banter" which was often sexist, misogynist and homophobic' (page X). Following Phipps and Young's research, the NUS (2014) conducted a study of men and women students' experiences of lad culture in higher education, which indicated that a significant number of them had witnessed the perpetration of physical and sexualised harassment and assault in and around their institutions, as well as being victimised themselves. Thus, in research, sexual harassment and violence have become more recognisable as pervasive features of what students experience as lad culture, and research has contributed to a more developed theorisation of laddish practices (as discussed in Phipps et al., 2018).

However, none of this small but important body of research on lad culture in higher education has explored staff perspectives. Thus, our project – upon which this book is based – was the first to do so. It is vital to consider staff perspectives for several reasons. First, staff are an important part of the university community; they can ignore, exacerbate, or challenge lad culture. Indeed, one of the Universities UK Taskforce (2016, 58–59) recommendations is that universities 'take meaningful steps to embed into their human resources processes (such as contracts, training, inductions) measures to ensure staff understand the

8 *Introduction*

importance of fostering a zero-tolerance culture and are empowered to take responsibility for this'. We argue that part of this must involve developing a shared understanding of what constitutes lad culture, sexual harassment, and violence, and what underpin them. As we argue in this book, currently, while there is a large degree of consensus over certain aspects of lad culture, there are also important differences. Furthermore, certain understandings and conceptualisations of lad culture – which were dominant in our research – serve to reduce its visibility to staff; we discuss this in Chapter 2 (see also Jackson and Sundaram, 2018). A second reason for exploring staff perspectives is that they can usually offer longer-term perspectives than students, as most will work at an institution longer than an individual student will study there. Third, by talking with a wide variety of staff – porters, professors, security staff, welfare personnel, staff development staff, bar managers, and so on – it is possible to get perspectives from those who work across diverse contexts and experience varied parts of university life. This offers different and possibly broader perspectives than are offered by students alone. Overall, if staff (as well as students) are to be tasked with challenging lad culture as recommended by Universities UK, it is crucial to explore what they understand lad culture to be, who they think is laddish, where they think laddism is evident, what they consider causes it, and how it might be tackled. We explore these questions in this book.

Importantly, our exploration of these questions is relevant beyond UK higher education contexts, as we discuss in the next chapter. Although lad culture is a UK-specific term, behaviours that are seen to characterise it – especially sexism, sexual harassment, and violence – are certainly not specific to UK higher education. A recent survey of all 39 universities in Australia, for example, suggested that 51% of all university students were sexually harassed on at least one occasion in 2016 (Australian Human Rights Commission, 2017, 6). There has also been a lot of work conducted in the United States, especially on physical and sexualised violence by fraternity brothers against women on college campuses. Like laddism in the UK context, 'frat cultures' have been characterised and critiqued as involving a 'pack mentality' (e.g. Sanday, 2007), excessive alcohol consumption, and sexually harassing and abusive behaviours. Thus, although this book draws on research conducted in England, as we demonstrate in Chapter 1, it is closely related to, and is in dialogue with, research internationally. Furthermore, our theorising, discussions, and recommendations are of relevance to researchers, university staff, policy makers, and students well beyond the shores of the United Kingdom. Our work also contributes to international debates, theories, and activism about sexism, sexual harassment, and violence beyond higher education, developing understanding of issues highlighted by, for example, activist work such as the Everyday Sexism Project and the #MeToo movement.

Our Research

Our research, which was funded by the Society for Research into Higher Education (SRHE), explored staff perceptions of lad culture in higher education contexts. There were four research questions.

1 In what ways are lad cultures manifest in different higher education contexts?
2 Are these manifestations problematic and, if so, how?
3 Are universities working to tackle lad cultures and, if so, how?
4 Does more need to be done to tackle lad cultures in higher education and, if so, what?

We chose to explore staff perspectives for a number of reasons as mentioned earlier, including that: (a) they may offer perspectives that differ from (as well as share similarities with) those of students; (b) they are able to offer 'insider' insights about institutional responses (if any) to aspects of lad culture, as well as what policies or practices might be put in place; (c) we need to know how staff perceive and understand lad culture if they are to be tasked with challenging it; and (d) staff perspectives on lad culture, sexual harassment, and sexual violence can be considered to be constitutive and reflective of institutional cultures. Additionally, as noted, no research had focused on staff.

Before commencing the research, we sought and were granted ethical approval from the Universities where we are employed: Lancaster University and the University of York. We interviewed staff during 2014–2015 from across six universities in England. We confined our study to England because of differences in funding structures and policy frameworks between English universities and those in other parts of the United Kingdom. The six institutions were purposively selected on the basis of institution-level characteristics which tend to influence campus culture and student demographics (especially the socio-economic, age, and ethnic profiles of student intakes): pre/post-1992 status; campus/non-campus; and geography (north and south). There were six institutions in our sample. Three were post-1992 universities (ex-polytechnics) and were located in different regions of England: north-west, north-east, and south-east. The other three were research-intensive, pre-1992 universities, members of the Russell Group or 1994 Group (before its dissolution), and also located in the north-west, north-east, and south-east of England. Classifying universities as campus or non-campus is not straightforward. If we define as campus universities those that have university-owned buildings and spaces situated in one place, then three of our institutions would most likely be classed as campus universities (two of the pre-1992 group and one post-1992) (see, for example, The Student Room list of campus universities). Table 0.1 provides an overview of our six sample institutions.

10 *Introduction*

Table 0.1 Key Features of Our Six Universities

University	Pre- or post-1992	Campus or non-campus	Region in England
U1	Post-1992	Non-campus	North-east
U2	Post-1992	Non-campus	South-east
U3	Post-1992	Campus	North-west
U4	Pre-1992	Campus	South-east
U5	Pre-1992	Campus	North-east
U6	Pre-1992	Non-campus	North-west

At each institution we conducted around ten interviews; most of these were individual ones (62 in total) plus three focus group discussions (each with three or four people). In total, 72 staff took part in the individual or focus group interviews, of whom 51 identified as women and 21 as men. A range of staff were involved, including senior managers such as Pro-Vice Chancellors, College Provosts, and Deans of School; Student Union officers; lecturers; welfare tutors; college officers; bar managers; and security staff. Most interviews were carried out face-to-face although some were conducted by telephone. All were undertaken by the two authors (separately), using the same semi-structured interview schedule (see Appendix 1). The themes covered included understandings of the term lad culture; individuals and groups associated with lad culture; higher education contexts in which lad culture occurs; causes of lad culture; and institutional frameworks or policies for tackling it. Most interviews lasted for approximately one hour; they were audio-recorded and transcribed in full. The interview data were coded thematically using NVivo11. Development of the codes was undertaken by the authors/interviewers and informed by previous research, the research questions and themes emerging from the data. There were 11 main codes, for example, contexts of lad culture, addressing lad culture, of which seven had sub-codes and some of which were further subdivided. For example, contexts of lad culture had 14 sub-codes including clubs, halls of residence, social media. One of these – academic contexts – was further subdivided into four, including course/discipline differences and laddism: staff towards students. All names in this book are pseudonyms chosen by the authors; quotations are taken from individual interviews unless otherwise indicated.

As we discuss in Chapter 1, in line with most of the previous research on laddism, we conceptualise it as a particular way of 'doing gender'. While people of all genders can perform laddism, it is very strongly associated with men and masculinities, both in this and previous studies. Thus, our discussions in this book about laddish performances relate almost exclusively to men and masculinities, and discussions about women relate predominantly to the effects of lad culture on them. The

Introduction 11

main exception to this is in Chapter 3 – who are the lads? – where we critically explore perceptions about laddish women, or 'ladettes'. We consider how laddish women were constructed and perceived by our interviewees, and how gender informs the ways in which laddish performances were read, judged, and understood.

Book Overview

Chapter 1 frames our study in relation to existing research about lad culture and sexual harassment and violence in higher education. We suggest that although research in these spheres is still relatively nascent in the United Kingdom, it provides an essential foundation upon which to build our own research and theorising. The small but important body of work on lad culture in higher education suggests that lad culture is associated with sexism, sexual harassment, and violence. We argue that while lad culture is a UK-specific term, the particular performance of masculinity associated with being a 'lad' is certainly not confined to the United Kingdom. Thus, we move beyond the United Kingdom to discuss related concepts and research internationally, drawing in particular on work on sexual harassment and violence conducted in the United States, noting also the similarities and differences between UK lad culture and United States frat and bro cultures. In doing so we demonstrate how our UK-based research is related to, in dialogue with, of relevance to, and has implications for, work internationally. We suggest that lad culture is a significant problem in and beyond the United Kingdom that needs addressing. We argue that in order to best understand and challenge lad culture, we need to acknowledge that it is gendered and theorise it in relation to masculinities, analysing as well the ways in which laddish masculinities intersect with other social categories, including social class, sexuality, ethnicity, and age. We explore strategies that have been employed to tackle lad culture and sexual harassment and violence in different national contexts, arguing that most are limited in their effectiveness as they have not explicitly conceptualised it as a structural gender issue.

In Chapter 2, we ask what is lad culture and where and how is it manifest in higher education? We begin by analysing the forms that lad culture can take, focusing first on lad culture in social spaces, exploring its associations with sexism and misogyny; sport and drinking (including initiations); homophobia and racism; and banter. We then move to consider laddism in teaching and learning contexts, exploring the ways it is performed by staff and students in these spaces. We argue that a fairly limited conceptualisation of lad culture renders it is less visible to some people, in some contexts, and that this act of invisibilisation is both political and related to practical constraints (as perceived by our participants). We propose that a different characterisation of lad culture

12 *Introduction*

may enable us to 'see' it as manifesting in multiple contexts, and to understand the less overt ways in which it might be enacted to harass, humiliate, intimidate, and degrade.

Chapter 3 explores staff views on who engages in lad culture, examining the intersections between gender, social class, ethnicity, and age as well as the spaces and contexts that are perceived to cultivate it. We argue that laddism is associated primarily with men and masculinities. However, interviewees also suggested that women can be laddish too, and in a small minority of cases they suggested that women are 'even worse' than men. We explore these views in depth and suggest that laddism is performed very differently by women and men. We argue that while laddish women were sometimes judged more harshly than laddish men, this does not reflect the behaviours of the women. Rather, such judgements about women expose the operation of pernicious gender double-standards, and reflect the notion that laddish women transgress gender norms while laddish men reinforce them.

We then consider social class, noting that in *social* contexts laddism was seen to be performed by middle- and upper-class young men whose entitled approaches meant they did not expect to be held accountable for their behaviours, they knew how to play the system, and they relied on their parents to bail them out. We refer to this as a discourse of entitled immunity, which was particularly evident in relation to men's rugby union teams who were seen to epitomise laddism. Laddism in teaching/learning contexts – in the form of disruptions and lack of engagement – was seen to be performed more commonly by 'non-traditional' students. We end the chapter by considering ethnicity and age (where we also discuss laddish staff), observing that laddism was most strongly associated with young, white, British men.

In Chapter 4 we analyse and explore the varied ways in which staff narrated explanations for men's laddism, noting that none included any explicit discussion about sexual violence. We argue that the vast majority of explanations for laddism lacked any gendered analysis and instead referred to peer group influences and the need to fit in, (in)authenticity, 'banter', age/maturity, effects of alcohol and/or the freedom afforded by a university context. Indeed, authenticity is a major theme in the first part of the chapter. Our analyses suggest that interviewees who mentioned gender either tended to essentialise laddism as 'boys will be boys' or, conversely, suggest that 'it's only banter, they don't really mean it'. We are critical of both types of explanation as they serve to trivialise and essentialise laddism and reduce men's accountability. We first scrutinise explanations for lad culture in social spaces and then consider teaching/learning contexts. Finally, we explore gendered analyses relating to power and competition; very few interviewees offered such analyses, those who did had professional or personal interests in gender, equality, and diversity.

Introduction 13

Chapter 5 contributes towards a (re)theorisation of lad culture that takes into account the hegemony of binary gender relations, the multiple and intersecting ways in which gender is performed, and the role of gendered organisational regimes of higher education institutions in fostering particular values. We argue that the maintenance of binary gender relations, including the sexual and social subjugation of women, is key to the perpetuation of lad culture. However, we argue that such features and mechanisms are frequently obfuscated by the dominant gender-blind analyses which we discuss and critique in Chapter 4. Thus, we present a reconceptualisation of lad culture that makes visible the gendered norms and expectations that underpin it, and takes into account the ways these intersect with other structural inequalities in specific contexts. In the final part of the chapter we draw on our (re)theorisation of lad culture to critically explore what is being done, and what should be done, to address lad culture in universities.

In the Conclusion we draw together our analyses and represent our main argument. We end by considering whether the term lad culture has value or whether we should be attempting to shift the conceptual terrain.

Notes

1 For ease of reading we do not use quotation marks around the term lad culture. However, we do recognise and want to emphasise the limitations of this term as well as problematise it, which we do in the book's conclusion.
2 The NUS is a confederation of around 600 Students' Unions in the United Kingdom. This confederation amounts to more than 95% of higher and further education unions in the United Kingdom. The NUS represents the interests of more than seven million students (www.nus.org.uk/en/who-we-are/what-we-do/).
3 We use the terms lad culture, laddish, and laddism interchangeably throughout this book.
4 By 'discourse' we mean

> groups of statements which structure the way a thing is thought, and the way we act on the basis of that thinking. In other words, discourse is a particular knowledge about the world which shapes how the world is understood and how things are done in it.
>
> (Rose, 2001, 136)

1 'Show Us Your Tits and We'll Buy you Shots'
Lad Culture, Sexual Harassment and Violence in Higher Education

Introduction

In this chapter we explore lad culture in higher education based on existing research in the United Kingdom and across international contexts. We recognise that lad culture is a UK-specific term, but that the attitudes and behaviours associated with it – including sexism, sexual harassment and violence – are not UK-specific. Thus, we pay particular attention to the similarities and variations in the manifestations of UK lad culture and its international equivalents, notably US bro culture and frat culture. We also explore the links between understandings and conceptualisations of lad culture/frat culture in higher education and national-level responses to addressing them. In discussing this relationship, we set the scene for our own research – explored in Chapter 2 onwards – which examines the perspectives and experiences of staff working in universities in England, and contributes to knowledge about the characteristics of lad culture, explanations for it, and enablers and barriers to prevention.

Understanding how lad culture has been discussed and analysed in previous studies gives us important insights into key aspects of the phenomenon: its forms, locations, and prevalence in university contexts, whether it is perceived to be gender-specific, and how institutions respond to it. It also helps us to consider whether lad culture might be described as a global phenomenon or whether it is specific to certain cultural contexts or specific sectors. In this chapter, we draw primarily on research from the United Kingdom and the United States as this is where the bulk of the published research has taken place; where available we also highlight work from other countries in which research on sexual harassment and violence in universities has been conducted, for example, Australia and Canada. We build a picture of the ways that lad culture (or its equivalent) has been described and delineate the key factors associated with it, including alcohol consumption, sport, and specific university communities. Of course, the way in which a problem is conceptualised and understood drives responses to it. For example, as we have argued elsewhere, if sexual harassment and violence are regarded as problems located at the individual level, and associated only with a 'few

Lad Culture in Higher Education 15

bad apples' or 'sex pests', the response to it will be very different than if it is seen to be a widespread cultural and structural problem underpinned by gender inequality (Jackson and Sundaram, 2018; Sundaram and Jackson, 2018). Thus, university-level and national campaigns and policy initiatives to combat lad culture reflect much about its perceived causes, the factors that are seen to sustain it, and its most problematic aspects. They also reveal how and where responsibility is attributed for practices associated with lad culture.

We now consider research on lad culture in the United Kingdom, before moving to consider research internationally.

Research on Lad Culture in Higher Education in the United Kingdom

As discussed in the Introduction to this book, the notion of 'lads' in education is not a new one; it was first conceptualised by Paul Willis in his germinal (1977) work *Learning to Labour*. His ethnographic study was predominantly concerned with the disaffection and disengagement from school of a group of white, working-class young men who termed themselves 'the lads'. They defined their own sub-culture as one that prioritised 'having a laff'. Willis' narration of certain practices associated with 'the lads' – some of which might be described as anti-social – mirrors in numerous ways how lad culture has been presented more recently in popular culture: in so-called lads' mags (e.g. Maxim, Loaded), television programmes (e.g. Top Gear, Men Behaving Badly), and elements of popular music culture (e.g. Oasis). The emphasis is on having fun, not taking things too seriously and not worrying about how others might view or be impacted by the behaviour.

As also noted in the introductory chapter, the term lad culture has only recently been applied to higher education and associated with a set of practices or a culture within universities (Dempster, 2007; NUS, 2013). Thus, research on lad culture in UK higher education contexts is still in its infancy. There is a relatively small but important body of work in which the focus has been exclusively on students' perspectives about, and experiences of, laddism (Dempster, 2007, 2009, 2011; Warin and Dempster, 2007; NUS, 2013; Jackson, Dempster and Pollard, 2015; Phipps and Young, 2015a, 2015b; Lewis, Marine and Kenney, 2018; Jeffries, 2019; Stentiford, 2019; Diaz-Fernandez and Evans, 2019a). This work, spearheaded by Dempster's research in the early-to-mid-2000s, has explored how men and women students conceptualise, engage with, and are impacted by lad culture in UK university contexts. This body of research has highlighted several themes that are important for our own research and will be picked up at various points throughout this book. First, laddism is typically regarded by researchers to be a particular performance of masculinity that is most often performed by men.

16   Lad Culture in Higher Education

Second, laddishness is not one thing, but might best be conceptualised as a continuum of gendered practice (Dempster, 2007; Jeffries, 2019; Stentiford, 2019). Third, men's relationships with laddism are complex: men self-identify as 'lads' to varying degrees, and even those who do identify as lads often disassociate themselves from the more extreme forms, thus practising what Dempster (2007) refers to as 'laddishness by degree'. However, while many self-identified lads disassociate themselves from more extreme forms of laddism such as sexual violence, lad culture scaffolds this violence (Phipps and Young, 2015b; Lewis, Marine and Kenney, 2018). Fourth, not all men engage in laddish behaviours, but lad cultures can dominate in certain contexts (NUS, 2013). Fifth, lad culture is associated with *groups* of men, especially in social contexts. Finally, elements of lad culture that are portrayed as involving 'homosocial bonding', fun, and having a good time with friends are often presented in a positive light. Thus, lad culture is not viewed as uniformly negative. However, it is particularly associated with sport, alcohol consumption, sexual harassment, and 'banter' that is frequently sexist, misogynist, and homophobic. More extreme forms of laddism involve sexual violence (NUS, 2013).

The strong association between laddism and sexual harassment and violence means that it is useful to consider here not only the research that has focused specifically on laddism, but also that which has explored sexual harassment and violence more generally in higher education. In the United Kingdom there is limited work in both spheres and much of it has been driven by the National Union of Students (NUS). Their *Hidden Marks* study (NUS, 2010) explored women students' experiences of physical intimidation, fear, and verbal, sexualised, and physical harassment and violence. It generated survey responses from over 2,000 women students in higher education institutions across the United Kingdom, of whom two-thirds reported having experienced some form of verbal or non-verbal harassment in or around their institution. Thus, it was ground-breaking in highlighting that sexual harassment and assault are experienced frequently by women university students, and it also revealed the emotional and psychological impact of the *fear* of sexual harassment and assault for these women. One in seven women reported experiencing a 'serious' physical or sexual assault while at university and one-third reported sometimes feeling unsafe to visit university buildings after dark. It suggested that violence against women in university settings was occurring at rates similar to, or higher than, rates than among women in broadly the same age group in the general population (Phipps and Smith, 2012; UUK, 2016), and that fear of violence continues to restrict women's behaviour (as demonstrated by Hamner, 1988).

In 2012, the NUS commissioned a study into women students' experience of lad culture as a specific phenomenon, and some of the themes referred to earlier emerged from, or were reinforced by, this project. Based

Lad Culture in Higher Education 17

on interviews with 40 women from universities across England, the researchers – Alison Phipps and Isabel Young – described lad culture as:

> a group or 'pack' mentality residing in activities such as sport and heavy alcohol consumption, and 'banter' which was often sexist, misogynist and homophobic. It was also thought to be a sexualised culture which involved the objectification of women and rape supportive attitudes, and occasionally spilled over into sexual harassment and violence.
>
> (National Union of Students, 2013, 28)

In that NUS study, lad culture was found to encompass sexism more generally, as well as sexual harassment, physical intimidation, and assault. Thus, that piece of research was pivotal in connecting the small amount of research that already existed on lad culture (notably, Dempster, 2007, 2009, 2011) with research on sexual harassment and violence.

The NUS followed up that research in 2014 by conducting a lad culture and sexism survey that generated 2,156 responses and included men and women participants. The data suggested that students of all genders had experienced unwanted sexual advances (26% overall) but that many more women (37%) than men (12%) reported experiencing these. Just over one-third of the participants had witnessed other students being subjected to unwanted sexual comments about their body (36%) or unwanted sexual advances (36%), and almost two-thirds (62%) had heard rape or sexual assault 'jokes' being told at university. Rates were even higher in a survey published by the alcohol education charity, Drinkaware (2015). Their survey of just over 2,000 students across the United Kingdom revealed that 54% of 18-to-24-year-old women students (and 14% of men students) experienced sexual harassment on nights out. Of these women, half said that this is experienced most or every time they go out.

In the two most recent surveys – conducted by Revolt Sexual Assault and The Student Room (2018) and Brook (2019) – we again see high levels of sexual harassment and violence among UK university students and low levels of reporting. The survey by Revolt Sexual Assault and The Student Room (2018) generated just under 4,500 responses from students and recent graduates across 153 different institutions; 62% had experienced sexual violence: 70% of women students and 26% of men students. The rates of sexual violence were also very high for disabled students (73%) and non-binary students (61%). Only 6% of those who had experienced sexual harassment or sexual assault reported their experience to the university, with the main reasons for not reporting being thinking it was not serious enough (56%); feeling too ashamed (35%); and not knowing how to report it (29%). Sexual assault and harassment at university were regarded as having become normalised by 42% of respondents; 55% agreed that there are attitudes and behaviours that

18 Lad Culture in Higher Education

sexualise and objectify women; and 56% agreed that certain people believe they are entitled to have sex. Unsurprisingly, students reported significant impacts on self-confidence, mental health, studies, and social life as a result of experiencing sexual violence (see also Phipps and Smith, 2012).

The Brook survey (2019) which received 5,649 responses from UK university students – the largest response to date – revealed a similar pattern: a high proportion of students, especially women, experience sexual harassment and violence but very few report it. For example, their data suggest that almost half of the women in their sample (49%) said they were inappropriately touched but only 5% reported it. A quarter of women (26%) were sent unwanted sexually explicit messages but only 3% reported it. Women were more likely to experience unwanted sexual behaviours than men: 49% of women said they had been touched inappropriately compared with 3% of men.

In general, then, there is relatively small but growing body of research in the United Kingdom looking at lad culture and/or sexual harassment and violence in higher education (Phipps and Smith, 2012; UUK, 2016). The evidence available points to high levels of sexual harassment and violence and low levels of reporting. Fortunately, the increasing visibility of sexual harassment more generally, and within higher education specifically, is leading to more scrutiny and research in this sphere. This includes scrutiny not just of students' harassing and violent behaviours, but also recently of sexual misconduct by university staff towards students (Ahmed, 2017; Bull and Rye, 2018; Page, Bull and Chapman, 2019). This has garnered growing attention in mainstream media, although the research evidence is currently still sparse. One notable piece of research that focused specifically on staff-to-student sexual harassment and abuse is the *Power in the Academy* study (NUS, 2018) conducted by The NUS and The 1752 Group – a national research, lobbying, and consultancy organisation. Drawing on data from an online national survey that generated 1,839 responses from current and former students in UK higher education, plus four focus groups with a total of 15 students, this study found that sexual misconduct perpetrated by staff in universities is an issue of significance. Out of all 1,839 survey respondents, 752 (41%) had experienced at least one instance of sexualised behaviour from staff, while a further 94 (5%) were aware of someone they know experiencing this (p. 8). Again, the patterns are gendered. Overall, 60% of the 846 respondents who reported experiencing sexual misconduct stated that the perpetrator(s) of staff-student misconduct were men, while 14% of respondents reported a female perpetrator (p. 10). Although most of the discussion in this book is about lad culture among university students, we do touch upon lad culture among staff at various points, most notably in Chapter 2. This is one of many areas of work in this sphere that deserves further attention; as Page, Bull, and Chapman (2019, 1311) argue, the absence of research evidence about staff sexual misconduct in the United Kingdom is 'one of the factors that has contributed to making this issue invisible'.

Overall, there is increasing recognition in the United Kingdom that lad culture, which encompasses sexual harassment and violence, poses a serious risk to certain groups of students and needs to be tackled in and by universities. We now move beyond the United Kingdom to consider research on lad culture internationally.

Research on Lad Culture in Higher Education Internationally

Research on sexual harassment and violence in university settings has a much longer tradition in the United States than in the United Kingdom or elsewhere, although as Phipps (2018a) points out, the sexual victimisation of women students has been studied in many countries. Phipps and Smith (2012) note that sexual and gendered violence have been regarded as a major problem in the United States since the 1980s. Thus, considerably more research has been conducted in the United States and over a longer time period than in the United Kingdom (see, for example, Koss and Oros, 1982; Koss, Gidycz and Wisniewski, 1987) with some important work also being undertaken in Canada (for example, DeKeseredy and Kelly, 1993; DeKeseredy and Schwartz, 1997; DeKeseredy, Schwartz and Alvi, 2000). In the United States, the National Institute of Justice funded the *National College Women Sexual Victimisation Survey* in 1996; it found that between 20% and 25% of women university students would experience sexual victimisation before they graduated (Fisher, Cullen and Turner, 2000). The *Campus Sexual Assault* survey (Krebs et al., 2007) included women and men respondents and found that one in five undergraduate women students experienced sexual assault or attempted assault during their time at university. In a more recent survey in the United States, Cantor et al. (2015) found a similar prevalence of sexual victimisation among students of all genders (around one in five). Overall, studies suggest that the sexual assault prevalence for women on college campuses in the United States is between 19% and 25% (Lund and Thomas, 2015). While there has been attention to sexual harassment and assault in universities in the United States for the last three decades or so, it is now gaining increased attention. Lewis, Marine and Kenney (2018, 57) note that:

> While campus rape in the US has been an acknowledged reality for the last three decades, interest in the issue has piqued with the recent influx of highly visible student-generated lawsuits against colleges

20 *Lad Culture in Higher Education*

for mishandling reported rapes (Anderson, 2014; Bahr, 2014). In January 2014, a Presidential commission initiated by Barack Obama declared campus rape a national emergency in the US.

(White House Council on Women & Girls, 2014)

In the wake of increasing attention to sexual harassment and assault more generally, studies in universities in other countries are beginning to emerge, although these are still very limited in number. A notable example is a recent Australian study (Australian Human Rights Commission, 2017) which showed sexual harassment and violence to be prevalent in Australian universities, with 51% of students reporting at least one instance of sexual harassment in the course of a year, and nearly 7% reporting at least one sexual assault in 2015 or 2016. Over a quarter of respondents were sexually harassed in a university setting in 2016. Women were almost twice as likely as men to have been sexually harassed, and students who identified as bisexual, gay, lesbian, or homosexual were more likely than students who identified as heterosexual to have been sexually harassed. The gendered pattern of perpetration and victimisation noted earlier is repeated here: the vast majority of perpetrators were men and the victims women. The qualitative information generated by this national study showed that alcohol consumption and attitudes towards women were significant contributing factors to sexual harassment and sexual assault. Residential settings also present a risk factor for sexual harassment and assault: students were most likely to have been sexually assaulted in a university residence or a residence social event; this parallels findings from the United States about 'Frat Houses' which we discuss shortly. The spaces where sexual harassment and violence occur are crucial to consider. As we discuss in Chapters 2 and 4 of this book, differences between universities were identified in terms of their perceived conduciveness to lad culture and the risk of sexual harassment or assault. Teaching and learning spaces were also identified as settings for sexual harassment; this suggests that alcohol and partying are not necessary factors for lad culture, or practices associated with it, to occur. Sexual harassment by staff was also evident in the Australian study and, as highlighted in recent work in the UK context (NUS, 2018), power disparities were a significant risk factor in relation to sexual harassment and assault.

A focus on 'risk' factors is common in the research on sexual harassment and violence in higher education in the United States. Typically, the focus is on behaviours such as alcohol consumption or participation in team sports as explanatory or correlatory factors. A pattern of 'risk factors' for perpetration can be established across national contexts. Common factors associated with sexual harassment and assault are alcohol consumption, conservative gender attitudes or sexism, and abuses of power (e.g. in relation to staff-student sexual misconduct). An important consequence of the emphasis on risk factors is that programmes to

Lad Culture in Higher Education 21

challenge violence against women often focus on encouraging women students to minimise risk (a public health approach), for example by avoiding 'risky' situations (Marine and Nicolazzo, 2017). Furthermore, such programmes have focused on creating change at the individual level rather than addressing cultures of misogyny and sexism. A systematic review by DeGue et al. (2014) of prevention strategies for sexual violence perpetration revealed that fewer than 10% of programmes included content to address factors beyond the individual level (e.g. peer attitudes, social norms, organisational climate), and the vast majority were one-dimensional, very short (one-off sessions), and lacked strong theoretical frameworks. We pick up this discussion later in the chapter, as well as in Chapter 5, when we discuss strategies that have been adopted to address lad culture and sexual harassment and violence.

While some analysis of 'risk factors' is necessary, a focus only on those may render less visible the gendered, sexist, and misogynist masculine cultures that are associated with sexual harassment and violence (Jackson and Sundaram, 2018). Unfortunately, the majority of the research literature on sexual harassment and violence in higher education in the United States has not made masculinity or gender performativity a central focus of the analysis, or of prevention strategies. We argue that such an analysis is essential and that comparisons across international contexts are helpful in illuminating the ways in which masculinities and gender are core to understanding gender-based harassment and violence across international borders.

There is some work that explores masculinities in relation to sexual harassment and violence in US universities, although this is limited in scope and scale. Here, we draw particular comparisons between the UK's lad culture and what in the United States is termed 'bro culture' – and also 'frat culture' when specific to college (see later). Bro culture codifies a shared set of values, attributes, and attitudes among a particular 'type' of man. In common with lad culture, bro culture establishes a hierarchy among men in which certain types of men are subordinated and excluded from the 'pack'. The 'Bro Code', which is very similar to what Kimmel (2008) calls the 'guy code', not only lays out the expectations for men who self-define as 'bros' but also reveals the underpinning expectations around 'appropriate' masculine performances. For example, the Bro Code states that 'A Bro never cries' and that 'A Bro never wears pink underwear' and 'A Bro never rents a chick flick' [sic] (https://brocode.org). These examples illustrate how being a 'bro' involves a 'relentless repudiation of the feminine' (Kimmel, 2008, 45), much like university lad culture does, as we will see in later chapters. Avoiding femininity was also a marker of being a 'lad' in Jackson's work in secondary schools in England: boys frequently illustrated what lads would *not* do by referring to what girls do, for example, a lad would not play hopscotch, mess about with his hair, or play with Barbie (Jackson, 2003,

22 Lad Culture in Higher Education

587–588). Thus, 'lad' or 'bro' masculinity is constructed in opposition to, and as better than, femininity.

In addition, US bro culture and UK lad culture both centre on sexist language and practice, often involve heavy alcohol consumption (on the part of the perpetrator), and also sexual harassment and violence (Kimmel, 2008). A body of work in the United States has shown that fraternities are associated with a set of practices that frequently involve sexual harassment, sexual coercion, and assault (Martin and Hummer, 1989; Copenhaver and Grauerholz, 1991). Martin and Hummer's work (1989) demonstrated that the norms and cultures of fraternities were conducive to sexual coercion and assault, pointing in particular to the preoccupation with competition and superiority, loyalty and secrecy, ritualistic alcohol consumption, and sexist and objectifying language about women. There is a well-established association between sexual victimisation and access to alcohol and a 'party culture'; Fritner and Rubinson (1993) found that alcohol use was associated with sexual violence in university contexts and that fraternity members and members of sports teams were over-represented among perpetrators. Copenhaver and Grauerholz (1991) undertook research with sorority women in a large university in the United States. Their research revealed that 24% of respondents had experienced attempted rape and 17% had been raped. Significantly, almost half of the rapes occurred in a fraternity house and over half occurred either during a fraternity event or were perpetrated by fraternity members, thus supporting previous finding that fraternity cultures and practices are conducive to sexual coercion. More recent research continues to support findings that fraternities are primary sites for sexual violence perpetration and victimisation in US universities (Loh et al., 2005; Mazar and Kirkner, 2016; Seabrook, Ward and Giarccardi, 2018).

Frat culture is specifically analysed as a set of values and practices that are related to stereotypical expectations of masculinity and more conservative attitudes about gender roles, and those, in turn, establish rape-supportive belief systems (Loh et al., 2005, 1344). As Berkowitz (2004) has noted, even men who do not perpetrate sexual assault may subscribe to similar gender beliefs as those who do, thus contributing to a culture or social environment that excuses, trivialises, dismisses, or even glorifies sexual harassment and violence. Armstrong, Hamilton, and Sweeney (2006) have also noted that sexual assault is an outcome of particular peer cultures focused on 'partying' and heavy alcohol consumption, combined with stereotypical expectations around male dominance and women's deference or acquiescence to men.

Drawing together findings from the United Kingdom and United States we suggest that lad culture and frat culture are most frequently characterised as encompassing excessive alcohol consumption, conservative or traditional expectations for men's and women's behaviour, sexist

Lad Culture in Higher Education 23

language and/or behaviour, sexual harassment, and sexual assault. These practices and attitudes are prevalent in university settings and are interlinked. While lad culture is a UK-specific term which is distinct from 'frat culture', there are clear commonalities (Diaz-Fernandez and Evans, 2019). Furthermore, frat culture, lad culture, sexual harassment, and assault are specifically gendered phenomena in terms of perpetration and victimisation patterns. The vast majority of people engaging in lad/frat culture and perpetrating harassment and assault are men, and the vast majority of those who are victimised are women.

A key difference between the United Kingdom and the United States in terms of contexts associated with lad culture/frat culture is the centrality of fraternities to lad/frat culture in the United States. Fraternities appear to provide a specific context in which certain practices are legitimised, including heavy and competitive drinking, initiations, derogatory language and treatment of women and other 'outsiders', and sexual harassment and coercion. The availability of physical space in which fraternity members congregate is also a distinctive feature of this community. While United Kingdom and Australian studies have shown that halls of residence are unsafe spaces for women, there is not one site or space in which lad culture is consistently more legitimated (although it may be more visible in some spaces than in others as we discuss in Chapters 2 and 5). In the United Kingdom and Australia, communities such as sports teams may be considered a 'high-risk' group for heavy drinking, disrespectful language and treatment of women, and sexual harassment. However, sports teams do not tend to be spatially distinct in the same way as fraternities, not all sports teams are valorised, nor do they receive subsidies in the same way as fraternities. Thus, attempts to tackle sexual harassment and violence need to be informed by the ways in which various cultures and spaces support and sustain it. Having argued that we need to focus on cultures of masculinities if we are to understand lad culture/bro culture/frat culture, we move now to outline how we theorise lad culture in this book.

Theorising Lad Culture

As research has shown that the primary perpetrators of laddism are young men, and the primary victims are women, lad culture has been theorised in the academic literature to be linked to particular constructions of gender and, in particular, to masculinity (Dempster, 2007; NUS, 2013) and sometimes specifically 'toxic masculinity' (Diaz-Fernandez and Evans, 2019, 1). We regard gender as performative and relational: masculinities and femininities are constructed through everyday discourse and in relation to each other. Laddism is a particular way of 'doing gender' and whilst men or women may perform laddism, it is strongly associated with men and masculinity. Furthermore, as we

24   *Lad Culture in Higher Education*

discuss in Chapter 3, the ways in which women and men 'do laddism', and are judged for it, are very different.

The attributes and characteristics associated with 'desirable' forms of masculinity shift over time and between cultural contexts; current analyses of lad culture therefore have to be seen as part of this shifting conceptualisation. The capitalist and consumerist 1980s were, for example, associated with competitive and individualist ideals where masculinity was embodied by power, authority, and dominance – 'hard body' masculinity as Jeffords (1984) termed it. This may have represented a deliberate rejection of the more androgynous masculinity of the 1960s and 1970s where a fluidity of gender performance was more explicit. Currently, research suggests that laddish masculinity has a great deal of social and cultural power within university contexts (and beyond) and is a template of hegemonic masculinity for contemporary young British men in higher education (Dempster, 2011; NUS, 2013).

Connell's (2005) concept of 'hegemonic masculinity' has been used to theorise how the most socially and culturally valued attributes, practices, and behaviours associated with men as a social group arise and are maintained. Hegemonic masculinity is tied to power and consent:

> it is what maintains the power of patriarchy, or the dominance of men as a class over women as a class. It is also crucial to the concept that hegemonic masculinity legitimates the mobilisation of power by consent: the dominant class is able to maintain its position because the subordinated have accepted its world-view, as instantiated through a taken-for-granted set of institutions and way of life.
>
> (Paechter, 2012, 231)

Although the concept of 'hegemonic masculinity' has been challenged on a number of fronts, it is still regarded by many as a useful concept and is widely used (Paechter, 2012; Phipps, 2017a). Hegemonic masculinity refers to the form of masculinity that is culturally exalted at any one time (Connell, 2005); it is a high status, dominant form of masculinity. Hegemonic masculinities are 'contextual constructs in that a particular form of masculinity acquires hegemonic status only in certain situations' (Mills, 2001, 21). It is an idealised form of masculinity that few boys or men can attain. Nevertheless, it is a standard against which masculinity is measured, and shapes understandings of what it means to be 'acceptably male'. Thus, it is constructed relationally, both in relation to other masculinities and to femininities. Although hegemonic masculinity varies across time and space, Connell notes that characteristics such as physical strength and size, aggression, limited-emotionality, competitiveness, and explicit displays of heterosexuality are highly valued and desired signifiers of masculinity in contemporary Western societies. As we explore in later chapters, these are also characteristics strongly associated with laddish masculinity in UK higher education environments.

Hence, we locate laddish masculinity as inextricably associated with hegemonic masculinity.

Connell's conceptualisation provides a valuable means to understand the values and attributes with which privilege is located and around which hierarchies of gender are established. However, as noted, this theorisation of masculinity captures the experiences of a relatively small group of men, and does not adequately represent the diverse ways in which masculinity is lived and enacted. For example, 1980s masculinity was represented and performed in many more varied ways than macho, tough, 'hard body' men. Neither does it adequately account for the increasingly diverse and fluid ways in which people are defining and experiencing gender (Renold et al., 2017). In recognising the complexity and fluidity of masculine performances, Hearn (2004) has argued that we must name the privileges and social, cultural, economic, and political power experienced by some men, the *hegemony of men* as a 'class', while acknowledging that not all men benefit from this patriarchal dividend in equal ways or measure. Thus, while laddism may be performed most easily by men who (can) embody hegemonic masculinity, it is far from all men who engage with these practices or who benefit from them. Laddish values and practices have been attributed primarily to heterosexual, white, cis men, who arguably hold the majority share of power and privilege in contemporary society, although within this group intersections of social class, sexuality, and dis/ability locate some men in more privileged positions than others. We explore these intersections in our analyses.

Conceptualising laddish masculinity as a particular performance of gender, or way of 'doing gender', also allows us to recognise and acknowledge that women may also perform 'laddishly', and we discuss this in Chapter 3 (see also Jackson, 2006b; Jackson and Tinkler, 2007). However, the strong association between masculinity (or masculinities) and lad culture helps us to understand how and why it is a gendered phenomenon, that is, why it is men who primarily engage with these practices and the values and performances that underpin them. It also allows us to analyse the particular gendered practices associated with lad culture as performances of masculinity. For example, the work of Dempster (2007) and others (Harnett et al., 2000; de Visser and Smith, 2007) has highlighted that drinking is regarded as a measure of what makes a man, and competitive drinking is a core aspect of laddish behaviour. Understanding laddism as a way of 'doing gender' also has implications for how to tackle it.

What Has Been Done to Address Lad Culture in Different Contexts?

Lad culture is clearly associated with a specific set of behaviours, factors, and practices. However, the way in which lad culture is understood, or conceptualised, varies. Furthermore, the ways in which it is

26   Lad Culture in Higher Education

conceptualised shape responses to it. The association of lad culture, including sexual harassment and violence, with specific behavioural factors – such as heavy or frequent alcohol consumption, participation in team sports, fraternity settings – has historically led to a symptom-focused response. Individuals or individual groups have been punished for 'one-off' incidents and there has been a lack of a system-wide approach to prevention. Furthermore, recent national policy initiatives to tackle sexual harassment and violence in universities have not explicitly conceptualised it as a gender issue.

As our own research suggests, there appears to be little institutional understanding of the gender basis of lad culture more broadly, or of sexual harassment and violence specifically. As we have already discussed, in the United Kingdom the impetus for addressing lad culture and violence against women in higher education has been driven by the NUS. Their work began to reveal the extent and impact of lad culture on women students in UK universities. More broadly, the Conservative-Liberal Democrat Coalition Government (2010–2015) launched an Action Plan in 2012, *A call to end violence against women and girls* (HM Government, 2012), which was followed by an updated strategy in March 2016 (HM Government, 2016) and another in 2019 (HM Government, 2019). The 2016 strategy (but interestingly, not the 2019 one) made reference to the newly established Universities UK (UUK) Taskforce which was charged with examining violence against women, harassment, and hate crime affecting university students. That Taskforce has been responsible for developing and implementing policy and guidance to higher education institutions for preventing and dealing with lad culture, sexual harassment, and violence. The Taskforce authored the *Changing the Culture* report in 2016 which outlined the policy context and evidence around violence against women, harassment, and hate crime in universities, and made recommendations for best practice for universities to adopt in tackling these issues. The report noted that most universities do not have specific policies to deal with sexual harassment or violence, and that they are dealt with under more generic bullying guidance which is not fit for purpose when it comes to receiving disclosures and supporting survivors of sexual harassment and violence. The UUK Taskforce also noted that there is a lack of centralised reporting systems for survivors and that the establishment of these would increase survivors' confidence in the institutional response.

The UUK Taskforce report acknowledged that violence against women and harassment are gendered phenomena. However, their recommendations for implementing improved reporting systems and policies for supporting survivors, and/or for preventing violence and harassment, do not draw on the wider research literature about the causes and impacts of gender-based harassment and violence against women. The language of 'unacceptable behaviour' and 'zero-tolerance approaches' (UUK, 2016,

Lad Culture in Higher Education   27

35) is used, but without making discursively visible the gender-specific nature of these behaviours or the values and practices that university communities should cease to tolerate. Explicit naming of women as the primary victims of sexual harassment and violence tends to occur in relation to 'honour-based' violence, such as forced marriage. Therefore, the UUK Taskforce report, while representing a landmark recognition of sexual harassment and violence in universities, tends to discursively render these issues as gender-neutral or, at least, as unrelated to gender norms and expectations. This means that the Taskforce does not highlight the need to tackle gender norms and expectations as a crucial aspect of violence prevention. In our view, this is a lost opportunity.

However, more positively, key to the UUK Taskforce recommendations for tackling sexual violence in universities is the adoption of a whole-institution approach for culture change. This is to be welcomed and represents an explicit move away from the more reactive, individually focused interventions that have characterised previous university responses to sexual violence. The culture-change approach has been developed and advocated by key researchers in the field in the United Kingdom, who have argued for challenges to the dominant individualised and competitive values of higher education (see: https://chucl. com/). The culture change framework emphasises the transformation of existing university cultures, which can be conceived of as reproducing hierarchy and inequality in a number of cross-cutting ways, and which therefore might enable and sustain gender-based harassment and abuse. The Changing University Cultures Collective (CHUCL) (https://chucl. com/) emphasises the need for greater social and political consciousness, empathy, and honest communication as fundamental to achieving institutional culture change. The UUK Taskforce report makes multiple reference to the work of the White House Task Force in the United States, where close collaboration with local police and the legal obligations of universities are emphasised. Conversely, the CHUCL approach represents a substantive shift away from a more criminological or legalistic framing of sexual violence in universities to thinking about building emotional intelligence and political consciousness across institutions.

In contrast, the US approach to addressing sexual violence and harassment in universities is characterised more explicitly by a legalistic approach and higher education institutions are required under Title IX and the Clery Act (1990) to address sexual violence on campus. The Title IX ruling of the 1972 Education Amendments protects people from discrimination on the basis of gender in education programmes or activities. Key issues that are covered by Title IX obligations include admissions, sports, the status of parent or pregnant students, and 'sexbased [sic] harassment' (https://www2.ed.gov/about/offices/list/ocr/docs/tix_dis.html). Most universities in the United States have Title IX Offices that are responsible for investigating complaints and supporting

28   Lad Culture in Higher Education

survivors. The Clery Act obliges universities to signpost survivors to counselling resources, to notify them of reporting mechanisms, and to make adjustments to accommodation and living conditions if this is requested. Title IX links governmental funding assistance to educational institutions' compliance with this law, thus representing a more developed mechanism for holding education institutions accountable in terms of their responses to disclosures of sexual harassment and violence. Under the Obama administration, and following high-profile mishandlings of sexual assault complaints at Harvard and Princeton Universities, nationwide guidance was issued to universities regarding their obligation to investigate sexual assault reports under Title IX. More recently, under the Trump administration, there has been some governmental resistance to the policy as it is currently implemented. Betsy DeVos, Republican Secretary of Education, has expressed concern about the fate of accused students and the perceived risk that false allegations may be encouraged by the way Title IX is taken forward in some universities. Her revisions to the guidance for educational institutions' responses to sexual harassment and violence have made it more difficult for survivors to report, *inter* alia by narrowing the definition of sexual harassment and allowing universities to ask for more evidence to substantiate complaints of sexual harassment and violence specifically (Department of Education, 2018). There has also been resistance to universities themselves dealing with complaints of sexual assault, and proposals for these cases to be forwarded to the police, with or without the survivor's consent.

Within the US context of a more legalistic approach to dealing with sexual assault complaints, non-governmental organisations, such as End Rape on Campus, are supporting and advising students on how to file complaints, how to access legal aid, the rights of survivors under Title IX, and where to access counselling and mental health support. Other initiatives that have been developed in the United States to address sexual violence include the Centers for Disease Control and Prevention (CDC) *STOP SV* package. The package includes programmes such as *Safe Dates, Green Dot, Coaching Boys into Men*, and *Bringing in the Bystander*. Within this package Bystander intervention is emphasised as a key means of transforming social norms and achieving the culture change that is necessary for preventing violence. The *STOP SV* package talks about 'creating protective environments' *inter alia* through improving safety in schools and in workplaces. A strand of the programme is also focused on teaching skills to prevent sexual violence in *school* settings. This represents a different approach from the one taken in higher education settings as the emphasis in schools is on education, and changing community or social norms, rather than having a legalistic bent. These school- or community-based education programmes have been evaluated and found to be effective in reducing acceptance of violence and developing anger-management skills. There have also been

Lad Culture in Higher Education   29

a few restorative justice approaches to sexual harassment and assault on university campuses (Coker, 2018). A sector-wide recommendation or approach to addressing sexual violence in universities does not exist in the United States, and there are wide variations in engagement with programmes in different states and universities.

At university level, the *Bringing in the Bystander* programme is perhaps the best known initiative to tackle sexual violence. This is mirrored in the United Kingdom, largely because the UUK Task Force recommended that universities should adopt a bystander intervention programme (UUK, 2016); we return to this in Chapter 5. The US programme has been found to be successful in reducing rape myth acceptance and to increase confidence in intervening in situations of sexual or physical partner violence among university students (Banyard et al., 2007). While gender stereotyping is addressed as a single component of some of these programmes, the fundamental link between gender norms and expectations, cultural contexts of gender inequality, and sexual harassment and violence is not fully explored in any of them. The notion that *individuals* are responsible for social norms change supersedes the notion that gender inequality is embedded into educational settings at multiple levels and in multiple forms. We deal with the institutionalisation of gender inequality and the ways in which this creates a conducive context for gender-based harassment and violence in Chapter 5.

Locating the Present Study

The questions that our study sought to answer focused on institutional perspectives and understandings of lad culture, with a view to illuminating cultural and structural enablers and barriers to prevention. There remains a dearth of knowledge about how university cultures enable sexual harassment and violence, and also about the perspectives and understandings of staff about these issues. We still have relatively little knowledge about the intersections between various forms of violence, including gender-based violence and racist, homophobic, transphobic, and disablist harassment, and abuse. While this book cannot – and does not attempt to – explore these intersections in depth, it does provide the first analysis of institutional perspectives on and encounters with lad culture. This allows us to answer fundamental questions about staff awareness, staff understandings, and institutional responses regarding lad culture.

In the United Kingdom, existing policy initiatives and interventions to deal with harassment and violence in higher education are limited as they are frequently developed on a weak evidence base. Research on the underlying causes of sexual harassment and violence is seldom used in the development of policy initiatives. To date, few training or other interventions to address sexual harassment and violence in

30 Lad Culture in Higher Education

universities have been robustly theorised or evaluated. A consistent approach to prevention in universities – informed and underpinned by well-established evidence around the causes, reinforcing factors (e.g. myths and misperceptions about sexual harassment and violence), and impacts of violence – has not been developed or implemented in the United Kingdom. The current UK policy framework for addressing sexual harassment and violence in higher education emphasises culture change as a means for prevention. However, understandings of the barriers to culture change remain very limited.

In the United States only Title IX and the Clery Act are mandated at federal level. The application of Title IX has been further deregulated by the US Government, which may lead to even less consistency in dealing with disclosures and supporting survivors in higher education settings. The current framework for responding to sexual harassment and violence in universities in the United States is focused heavily on reporting and prosecuting, and has been criticised for failing to bring about behaviour and culture change (e.g. Collins, 2016). As noted earlier, while several programmes for promoting behavioural change have been developed and evaluated, these are not implemented at the federal, or even state, level. Collins (2016, 366) notes that the dominant legalistic approach necessitated a partnership between violence against women scholars and activists, and more conservative actors who sought to increase punitive state policies. This framework has led to a privileging of some types of victims over others; some victims are constructed as more 'deserving' of support and retribution than others, while others are cast as more 'deserving' of violence.

Richardson and May's (1999) analysis of who constitutes 'deserving' victims of violence is closely linked to questions about institutional and cultural barriers to challenging violence against women. The ways in which victims are read, believed (or not), and responded to by staff working in universities are key to understanding how institutions support survivors and seek to prevent and challenge sexual harassment and violence. As Richardson and May (1999) note, the characteristics of the victim, the circumstances in which the violence occurred, the characteristics of the perpetrator, and the contexts in which violence occurs all contribute to the notion of 'deservedness' – the extent to which a person 'deserves' or may be held accountable for the violence they experience. Myths about how violence takes place, what harassment and violence 'look like', and who typical perpetrators are all shape constructions of who 'deserving' victims are. Intersections between gender, sexuality, social class, ethnicity, dis/ability, and age are all influential in constructions of 'deserving' or 'undeserving' victims, and in judgements about which lives matter (Richardson and May, 1999).

Therefore, it is imperative to uncover the ways in which these views are constructed in order to understand the cultural and institutional

Lad Culture in Higher Education   31

reluctance to empathise with, and to believe, all survivors of sexual harassment and violence. The construction and identification of survivors as 'deserving' or not are intimately linked to gender expectations and norms. Stanko's (1990, 49) observation that 'if people frequent places that are known to be dangerous or they do not follow exactly the rules for precaution then we implicitly hold them responsible for whatever happens to them' remains highly relevant to the ways in which women are held accountable for violence perpetrated against them. The recent case of Ford versus Kavanaugh in the United States clearly highlights the ways in which women are expected to behave in particular ways in order to be believable as 'deserving' victims. In this case, Ford, a well-respected university professor, holds significantly more privilege than other women who have experienced assault, yet her credibility and her *innocence* (i.e. her non-deservedness) remain under intense scrutiny and suspicion – even by the current president himself (www.bbc.co.uk/news/world-us-canada-45727618). Existing research with much younger people shows that gender norms are fundamental in their acceptance of violence towards girls and women, and that the behaviour of the (female) victim and the extent to which this behaviour is seen as transgressing gender norms are central factors in their accounts of violence as acceptable or deserved (McCarry, 2010; Sundaram, 2014). Sundaram (2014, 73) argues that:

> Women who had been unfaithful to their male partners, women who did not do what their male partners asked them to do, women who had lied to their male partners and sexual rejection of a male partner were all narrated as scenarios in which normative gender behaviour had been transgressed and violence might (understandably) be used.

Policies and interventions to challenge sexual harassment and violence in university settings therefore need to be informed by an understanding of how survivors are viewed and how gender expectations intersect with institutional understandings of, and responses to, victim-survivors.

This book explores perspectives of staff working in higher education about lad culture, sexual harassment, and sexual violence. We examine their understandings of what constitutes problematic behaviour, who perpetrates these behaviours, and their explanations about why such behaviours occur. The findings enable us to identify the barriers within and across higher education institutions that conceal, dismiss, and trivialise sexual harassment and violence. Given that survivors of sexual harassment and violence are dependent on key change-makers and power-holders within universities to believe them, to understand the impacts of their experiences, and to view them as 'deserving' of empathy and support, it is crucial that obstacles to engaging these key stakeholders are identified. The book therefore contributes to the existing field

32 *Lad Culture in Higher Education*

by, among other things, pointing to key enablers and barriers to culture change at the institutional level, and identifying the factors that must be considered and addressed if frameworks for gender-based violence prevention in universities in the United Kingdom and elsewhere are to be effective.

Summary

In this chapter we explored existing research about lad culture and sexual harassment and violence in higher education. We noted that although research in these spheres is not extensive in the United Kingdom, it provides an essential foundation upon which to build our own research and theorising. We discussed research conducted outside of the United Kingdom, drawing in particular on work on sexual harassment and violence in the United States, and noting the similarities and differences between UK lad culture and US frat and bro cultures. We argued that lad culture is a significant problem in and beyond the United Kingdom and it needs addressing by universities. We suggested that in order to best understand and challenge lad culture, we need to acknowledge that it is gendered and to theorise it in relation to masculinities, analysing as well the ways in which laddish masculinities intersect with other social categories including social class, sexuality, ethnicity, and age. We move now to focus on our own research which explored the perspectives of staff in six universities in England about lad culture. We start our detailed exploration in the next chapter by investigating what lad culture looks like in higher education in England.

2 'But Most of It's Banter'

What Does Lad Culture Look like in Higher Education in England?

Introduction

The key questions we address in this chapter are what is lad culture, and where and how is it manifest in higher education in England? To address these questions we analyse university staff narratives about the different forms that lad culture, or laddish behaviour, can take. Drawing on our interviews with a diverse range of staff across six institutions in England, we explore how lad culture is characterised. We argue that lad culture encompasses a range of practices that we regard as underpinned by gender-based harassment and abuse. However, the discourses that staff draw on to describe, explain, and at times rationalise lad culture reveal clearly stratified understandings of who is a lad and what laddish behaviour encompasses. We analyse the ways in which harassment and abuse are invisibilised through such stratified conceptualisations, and argue for a fuller characterisation of lad culture – including the spaces in which it is enacted – in order to clearly identify and challenge harassment and abuse when it occurs. This analysis has implications for the ways in which laddism and lad culture are represented and problematised (or not) in educational (and other) discourse.

We start by analysing the forms that lad culture can take in higher education, paying particular attention to underpinning themes that cut across them. We focus first on lad culture in social spaces, exploring its associations with sexism and misogyny; sport (including initiations) and drinking; homophobia and racism; and banter. We then move to consider laddism in teaching and learning contexts, exploring the ways it is performed by staff and students in these spaces.

Finally, we make the argument that a limited conceptualisation of lad culture can render it is less visible to some people, in some contexts, and that this act of invisibilisation is both political and related to practical constraints (as perceived by our participants). We argue that a broader (but precise) characterisation of lad culture may enable us to 'see' it as manifesting in multiple contexts, and to understand the less overt ways in which it might be enacted to harass, humiliate, intimidate, or degrade. This analysis is directly related to participants' understandings of who 'the lads' are (Chapter 3), and how lad culture should be tackled (Chapter 5).

What Is Lad Culture?

> I think really the short answer is a real hegemonic masculine approach to life, but with a particular emphasis on booze, drugs, sex and sport from the middle-class white male perspective.
>
> (Jessica, woman, U2)

Lad culture was a familiar and recognisable notion to most but not all of our participants. Those who had heard about, witnessed, or experienced lad culture defined the practices and attitudes associated with it in varying ways, although there was a large degree of consensus about core aspects of it.

As we have argued elsewhere (Jackson and Sundaram, 2018) there were many parallels between the ways our interviewees described laddism and the way it has been conceptualised and presented in the media. For example, laddism has been presented in the UK press largely in relation to students' social lives, and most staff focused on this sphere, at least initially. Furthermore, reports about lad culture in the media have highlighted 'extreme' manifestations of laddish behaviour that are more likely to cause moral outrage and, as we discuss later, some of our interviewees also tended to conceptualise laddism as extreme. We recognise that there are plenty of examples of 'extreme' laddism. However, representing lad culture only as extreme tends to go hand-in-hand with portraying it as rare and perpetrated only by a 'few bad apples' who are easily identifiable. Such portrayals tend to render invisible lad culture's entanglements with other sexist practices and with wider social and cultural norms for gender behaviour. They work to pathologise a small number of 'extreme lads' and render invisible the broader sociopolitical discourses that normalise sexism and harassment as part of everyday life. Thus, in our analyses we were mindful of the ways in which the current representation and conceptualisation of lad culture in, for example, the mainstream media related to its conceptualisation and in/visibility in university settings. A continued absence from press reports is an analysis of the underpinning culture of gender inequality and misogyny within these university contexts. As we discuss, media-led discourses about university lad culture may have contributed to a silencing or invisibilising of the pervasive sexism, harassment, and violence within university communities themselves. The visibility or invisibility of lad culture was very much linked to how staff conceptualised it (Jackson and Sundaram, 2018), and we explore that relationship later in this chapter.

Staff who were familiar with the term lad culture, and these were the vast majority, provided a plethora of instances – based on occurrences they had witnessed or events that had been relayed to them by others – of what they considered it to be. Examples spanned a range of contexts and were frequently typified by sexism and misogyny, and also but less frequently by homophobia and racism. As in Phipps and Young's research (NUS, 2013) lad culture was conceptualised as a 'pack mentality' although laddish behaviour could be performed by individuals; it was also strongly associated with sport and heavy drinking. These associations meant that it was thought to be most common in social spaces, although as we discuss later, there were also many reported instances of laddism in teaching and learning contexts, especially in some of the universities. We begin by exploring sexism and misogyny.

Sexism and Misogyny

Sexism and misogyny were identified as core elements of laddish behaviour by our participants.

> I think sexism is the most dominant element of lad culture. I certainly think there are elements of racism and homophobia in there but I think generally actually they are seen as less acceptable - homophobia and racism in our society generally - so I think they're a slightly less acceptable element of lad culture but they're certainly still an element of it.
>
> (Jessica, woman, U2)

> For me as a term it picks out more the sort of younger generation; a casual approach to, or disregard for, issues of gender equality, and perhaps sometimes quite overt sexism, even misogyny at times.
>
> (Daniel, man, U4)

A plethora of examples of laddism were provided by interviewees; these included physical, verbal, visual, and sexualised actions used to shame, demean, humiliate, objectify, and intimidate women students in relation to their gender, sexuality, and ethnicity. Our interviewees spoke of lad culture in ways that generally accord with the argument of Dempster (2007) and others (for example, Phipps and Young, 2015a) that laddism is not one thing, but rather is a constellation which in some ways might be regarded as a continuum: 'Well I suppose it can range from sexist comments, jokes, remarks that kind of thing, from one end of the spectrum to actually physical abusive behaviour' (Mary, woman, U6). Examples at the 'milder' end included sexist stereotyping: '[...] there's always one really moany person and it's always a woman and they act like this and all women are usually complaining...' (Kate, woman, U6). While towards the more extreme end they included objectification of women which involved sexually derogatory or demeaning language that drew on themes of sexual assault and physical violence.

> A couple of the girls had had their pictures cut out of the calendar and had things put next to them and posted up around the halls,

36 *What Does Lad Culture Look like?*

> like saying 'dress like this and you're asking to be raped' kind of thing. And you know, 'oh, no surprise you're at the front, you're a right slag!'
>
> (Rebecca, woman, U4)

Rebecca's example illustrates how normative gender expectations were invoked to shame women on the basis of their appearance, behaviour, and perceived promiscuity. This was a common theme: 'He [one of the rugby club boys] said something as he walked through the door like "the girl I took home last night had an implant in her arm so she must have been a slut"' (Claire, woman, U5). As in the earlier example from Rebecca, rape-trivialising discourses were fairly common. The pervasiveness of such discourses was thought to be rooted in, and to contribute to, a wider culture in which disrespect, abuse, and violence towards women were normalised and even glorified. Participants discussed the diverse settings in which they had witnessed sexist language and sexualised and degrading imagery and behaviour, including by construction workers on campuses, by university students on public transportation, and by staff in lecture theatres. Phipps and Young (NUS, 2013) also found that sexism, casual misogyny, and rape-supportive attitudes characterised women students' experiences of lad culture. Their participants defined campus cultures as gendered, making links between laddish practices and the 'cultural sexism' (Lewis, Marine and Kenney, 2018, 58) evident on their campuses. Thus, laddish individual (or group) practices were located within, and supported by, a specifically gendered cultural and social context.

Our interviewees also reported sexualised name-calling and humiliation, sexist chanting and intimidating shouting in public spaces, and sexual harassment in online spaces. Phipps et al. (2018) have noted the ways in which new mobile technologies enable different forms of expression of sexism and misogyny. Our interviewees cited a number of examples of misogynistic bullying on social media platforms and using mobile technologies, which again reinforced the centrality of gender-based harassment to these manifestations of lad culture.

> Our [anti-harassment] campaign started from Spotted in the Library. There have been very derogatory comments, mostly by blokes in the library and in the Learning Commons, about females that they'd spotted, what they looked like, describing what they'd like to do to them, all those kind of things.
>
> (Hannah, woman, U6)

Sending each other pictures of their conquests, either mid shag, or sometimes without them [women] knowing, which is very concerning [...] blokes circulating pictures of unconscious or just women who are not dressed at all, completely naked, who are not aware of the fact that a picture's been sent and it will be circulated around men. And what's really worrying is how acceptable that is amongst other men, completely acceptable.

(John, man, focus group, U5)

The use of sexist and sexually objectifying imagery in social spaces, including on university campuses, was fairly widespread. This was seen to contribute to the development of a cultural context that normalised sexually objectifying representations of women's bodies, and created problematic expectations about women's bodies and ways of interacting with them:

If advertising for the club nights or all the events are really like sexually objectifying women and that kind of stuff, it's quite intimidating and like pretty bad for your self-esteem and self-confidence. And it's typical, yeah I think it's quite negative.

(Chloe, woman, U6)

Although such images were evident in a host of contexts across campus, interviewees noted how publicity materials relating to the night-time economy were especially problematic.

Sexism and Misogyny in the Night-time Economy

A lot of nightclub promoters ... use lad culture quite obviously in their marketing.

(Rob, male, U3)

Our participants highlighted the ways in which universities, nightclubs, and events companies perpetuate and sanction aspects of lad culture through publicity materials and themed socials. Interviewees reported examples of publicity materials they had seen at Students' Union (SU) events or in university advertising which were sexist and used degrading or objectifying language and/or imagery, and in some cases promoted rape culture. Explicitly sexualised and sometimes misogynistic or homophobic text or images were used in marketing and publicity materials in university settings as well as off campus.

With club propaganda as well, like the lad culture is pervasive through that. Because like with [name of nightclub] they'll advertise their club by having a woman with a cap and a crop top and short shorts, just there anyway. It's this misogynistic, homophobic....

(Molly, woman, focus group, U5)

38 *What Does Lad Culture Look like?*

Such materials are certainly not specific to the universities in our sample; there have been some particularly shocking and disturbing examples, as highlighted by Diaz-Fernandez and Evans (2019a, 2):

> Drinking cultures are central to lad culture, evidenced by a widely publicised use of lad culture rhetoric in promotional material. Examples include Cardiff Metropolitan Student Union posters advertising Freshers events that featured a person whose t-shirt read 'I was raping a woman last night and she cried'. In 2013, Leeds-based events company Tequila UK promoted a themed nightclub event named 'Freshers Violation'. The video advertisement asked male students how they were going to 'violate' female students, with responses including 'fist them in the ass' and that women were 'gonna get raped'. While these examples provoked national condemnation, the use of sexist and objectifying images of women or sexualising 'themed' nights (e.g. pimps and hoes, sluts and geeks) have become a normalised part of the visual and spatial landscape of student nightlife.

In such instances, SU and universities are contributing to a cultural context in which particular representations of women, gender-based harassment, and violence towards women become normalised (see also Leathwood, 2013).

> It was brought to my attention recently that we have a rapper who is coming to play a gig next week who glorifies and kind of incites rape and violence against women and murdering women in his lyrics quite a lot. And that's happening and it's a sold-out gig in our union.
>
> (Kate, woman, U6)

> There's a night at the Student Union called Absolute Filth, so you can dress up in kind of the most horrendous outfit ever. And there's always a debate: actually should we be encouraging people to dress up like that? Because ... people start saying things and jokingly students will call each other, 'oh you slag', this and that as banter. But then it can go a bit too far and then all of a sudden people are like, actually that's not OK.
>
> (Rebecca, woman, U4)

In our interviews, staff who frequented student social spaces reported lad culture to be rife. These were almost exclusively SU staff; in other words, they were students who were taking time out of their degree to undertake an SU role for a year or so, or people who had very recently been students. These interviewees, who were mainly women, generally

What Does Lad Culture Look like? 39

saw lad culture as pervasive in student-frequented nightclubs and similar venues: 'this guy just walked up to her, unzipped her playsuit which then made it slip off her shoulders and revealed her bra, and stuck his hand down her pants' (Naomi, woman, U3). Indeed, unwanted sexual attention and touching were reported to be so ubiquitous that students saw it as normal; it was not something they talked about and certainly not something they reported. For example, as one SU officer from U3 told us:

ABBY: I would never think to report it to be honest. It's never, maybe it's because it's never really scared me enough for me to think it's a problem, but I mean it could be. Yes I've definitely been touched when I've said don't touch me, I've definitely had my skirt pulled up, I've definitely had people like kiss me when I've said get away from me, and they'll just take your face and they'll just kiss you. There's not a lot you can do about it, but I'd never ever think to report it.

INTERVIEWER: Why not?

ABBY: I don't know, this is the thing, I don't know and it's a good point. I wonder what stage it would have to get to to think I've got to report that. Maybe it's 'cos it's people I know, I'm not sure, I don't know.

INTERVIEWER: ... if you felt like you wanted to report it would you know how, and do you think that it would be taken seriously?

ABBY: I wouldn't know how. Taken seriously? I don't know because I've obviously not taken it seriously enough to report it, so maybe not. Like I say, I don't know what it would take to take it seriously. I've never been carried out of a club or down the street. It's always been in a club so I know I'm in the club ... it's like what would you say to report, 'cos I could give you 20 reports from one night out.

The ubiquity of sexual harassment is, ironically, one of the reasons Abby cites for not highlighting or reporting it. It is so commonplace that it is normalised. Thus, its ubiquity and normalisation contribute to its invisibility; it is not made visible to higher education institutions by students through complaints processes. In our research, as in Diaz-Fernandez and Evans' (2019a, 15) work, 'there was an overarching sense that these experiences were an inevitable component of student life' and that 'lad culture was all-pervasive and unavoidable'. Lad culture took on an explicitly gendered dimension in our research, with women identified as the primary targets of sexual harassment and assault which was perpetrated by men. In very few instances did participants mention sexual harassment being perpetrated by men against gay men students, and there was only one example of a woman harassing a man, which was dealt with very quickly and is discussed in Chapter 3.

40 *What Does Lad Culture Look like?*

> In clubs there are a lot of people physically, basically sexually assaulting women. Kind of going up and grabbing them and putting their hands up people's skirts, stuff like that, it happens a lot.
>
> (Kate, woman, U6)

> They see groups of lads in nightclubs and the sort of approaching women inappropriately and trying to grope them and that sort of thing. But they said that most girls they see are able to hold their own and give back as good as they get.
>
> (Michelle, woman, U3)

There is little evidence from our research or other studies to suggest that women 'give back as good as they get'. This is not to say that women do not find strategies to attempt to manage and/or avoid sexual harassment and violence, or to minimise the risk of 'serious' assault. On the contrary, there is a large body of work, including the Everyday Sexism Project (an international online project that collects women's stories of sexism, harassment, and violence), that demonstrates how 'women modify and restrict their own practices, language and movements in order to avoid — or to mitigate against the impacts of — sexual harassment and violence in public spaces' (Sundaram and Jackson, 2018, np). This is particularly heightened in spaces of the night-time economy where there are strong (masculinised) drinking cultures. Fear of violence in the night-time economy is high and women undertake a lot of work to mitigate the risks of harassment and violence, for example, drinking in 'safer' spaces and strategising with women drinking companions (Sheard, 2011; Diaz-Fernandez and Evans, 2019a). As Diaz-Fernandez and Evans (2019a, 3) suggest, women students negotiate lad culture in the night-time economy through 'neoliberal discourses of self-management'. Our findings echo theirs in this regard. Indeed, some of our interviewees who went to nightclubs told us about their strategies and how they varied depending on the day of the week, with Saturday being particularly dangerous. The ubiquity of sexual harassment, in particular, seemed to render it harder to challenge and in some instances meant that the focus of action shifted to self-monitoring and vigilance, for example, about what they wore, how much alcohol they had to drink, and so on.

> On a Saturday night not only is it [handbag] round me but it's on my front, it's not on my back. And my skirt's lower and I've got a lot less alcohol and I'm watching everyone more. And you've just got to be more vigilant because there are different people out there that act differently and are more persistent.
>
> (Abby, woman, U3)

What Does Lad Culture Look like? 41

Participants noted that sexual harassment and violence were very rarely reported to staff working in these social venues, often because of a perception that they would not be taken seriously: 'Because they expect the clubs to be a bit rubbish, and there are a lot of stories of people telling a bouncer or staff or whatever in clubs and people are like, "we can't do anything about it, sorry"' (Kate, woman, U6). Also, as noted earlier, students expected this type of behaviour, and the fact that it was so pervasive, frequent, and expected made it more difficult to report. Men's sports teams, especially football and rugby, were described by our participants as generating a particular 'affective atmosphere' (Diaz-Fernandez and Evans, 2019a) in social spaces, as we now explore.

Sport and Drinking

As in other studies on lad culture – both in higher education and secondary schooling – the majority of our interviewees closely associated lad culture with men's sports teams, especially, but not exclusively, the rugby and football clubs (Jackson, 2006a; Dempster, 2009, 2011; NUS, 2013; Nichols, 2018; Jeffries, 2019).

> Sport I think and drinking possibly, yeah, primarily I would have said … Because I think a lot of what I see as lad culture is kind of social practice that is around or focused on a either sport or being in the pub or that kind of stuff. So, yeah, I think those two things probably are the main characteristics.
>
> (Heather, woman, U6)

> It's a term [lad culture] that I would associate with sort of more groups of guys, sport, rowdy: 'what goes on tour stays on tour', that kind of lad culture would be what I would normally associate in my general day-to-day life.
>
> (Lucy, woman, U2)

As illustrated in the first quotation, the association of sport with lad culture was almost without exception also related to drinking cultures. There are long-standing associations between masculinity and both sport and drinking (Dempster, 2009, 2011). Indeed, Connell has described sport as the 'embodiment' of hegemonic masculinity (1995, 54). Thus, given our argument delineated in Chapter 1 about the hegemony of laddism as a form of masculinity in contemporary UK higher education, the strong associations between lad culture, sport, and drinking are unsurprising. Dempster's (2009) work conveys the ways in which men's sporting cultures emphasise and test hegemonic masculinity both on and off the pitch (see also Skelton, 1993). In his research as in ours

42　*What Does Lad Culture Look like?*

the off-pitch tests generally involved consuming copious amounts of alcohol and being 'up for fun' on the frequent team socials.

> I was part of the rugby team, so sexism and misogyny: it was pretty much that culture. One of the reasons why I stopped playing was because I couldn't be bothered with the: you have to go out and drink loads of beer and make a fool of yourself and if you don't you're not going to be part of the team.
>
> (Rob, man, U3)

As Rob narrates, team members must continually prove their masculinity to maintain a place on the team. However, to get a place on the team in the first instance, wannabe players often have to prove themselves in an initiation. So we focus next on initiations. In the next chapter we discuss, at length, the intersections of sport, especially rugby union, laddism, and social class.

Initiations

As in our research, Phipps and Young (NUS, 2013) found that student nights were contexts for gender-based harassment and abuse targeting both men and women students. In the case of the former, the emphasis was placed on rituals and activities that demanded a particular performance of masculinity to 'make it', to be seen as one of the team. Such rituals were particularly common when new members joined a team and had to prove, through an initiation ceremony, that they were worthy of a place. Such initiations are particularly associated with sports teams and fraternities in the United States, where they are referred to as 'hazing'. In the United States many students have died during hazing rituals, with over 30 deaths in the decade up to 2017, the overwhelming majority of whom were men (Time.com, 11 October 2017). The biggest cause of death is alcohol poisoning. While hazing or initiation rituals are particularly associated with colleges in the United States, they have also become increasingly common in the United Kingdom where there has also been several fatalities (NUS, 2013). Much like in the United States, initiations in the United Kingdom usually involve new members having to drink excessive amounts of alcohol and undertake humiliating, unpleasant, and often dangerous acts. In universities in our sample, team initiations had been banned formally, but there was recognition that they could and did still occur informally, often away from campus: 'the Students' Union doesn't allow it [initiation ceremonies] but of course local nightclubs have tried to get in on the act: oh we'll sponsor your sports team and you can drink here and you can have an initiation ceremony here' (William, man, U4). These initiations were strongly associated with laddism, and almost all of the accounts in our research involved the men's rugby club.

What Does Lad Culture Look like? 43

We're trying to work with the Students' Union. So they can't have initiations, but [we're] trying to get that balance because if you stop things then it just goes underground, then you don't know what happens. ... And we've had some quite dodgy initiations where they've had to, things that have been a bit more innocent, you know play rugby in your boxer shorts with a frozen turkey, to then kind of, they've acted out taking each other hostage in a car park and then the Vice Chancellor's gone past and thought it's a real life thing.

(Rebecca, woman, U4)

I've heard about the rugby initiation which wasn't supposed to happen this year, but entailed, they were kidnapped in a van, naked, the players, the new freshers, and they had to run down the [name of steep hill in the centre of the city] naked.

(Andy, man, focus group, U5)

They'd [the men's rugby club] managed to acquire a pig's head from somewhere and the combination of each individual's initiation was French kissing a pig's head. They were also doing, throwing people into a paddling pool full of bits of fish.

(Josh, man, U3)

I've heard stories of having to drink loads, swallow live fish, eat raw eggs, just making you throw up, a lot of nakedness. I think the rugby and hockey teams sometimes bring the boys' and the girls' teams together and make them do kind of, put first years in compromising positions, make them strip and all this kind of stuff. And I know that the [men's] rugby team, when I was in first year, I knew someone in the rugby team and his initiation was they were all blindfolded, taken to a basement somewhere in [name of city], made to drink ridiculous alcohol and strip naked. They wrote like an emergency phone number on their arm and then they just let them free in [name of city], a city that most of them had no idea about their way around, absolutely blind drunk. And basically the number was there if they ended up in hospital or were arrested which some of them did. Like find your way home kind of thing.

(Kate, woman, U6)

As Kimmel (2008, 99) argues, 'initiations are all about masculinity – testing it and proving it'. In our research, initiations worked to ensure the new recruits had the endurance, perseverance, and bravery that were viewed as necessary masculine qualities for team inclusion and were 'tested' through different acts of humiliation, punishment, and intimidation. Unless recruits could prove they were 'man enough' – mentally and physically tough and able to drink copious amounts of alcohol – they

44 *What Does Lad Culture Look like?*

would be excluded from the club. As we discuss in more fully in Chapter 3, rugby union is particularly noted for its role in shaping a particular class-specific form of masculinity in elite schools, characterised by discourses of 'aggression, ruthlessness, competitiveness and giving all for the school' (Light and Kirk, 2000, 167). Based on research in an elite school in Australia, Light and Kirk (2000, 168) note how proving their toughness was embedded into all aspects of the boys' rugby (union) training and day-to-day team life:

> ideals of suffering, sacrice and the toleration of physical pain were central to the development of the boys' masculinity. Within a dominant discourse of 'no pain no gain' physical pain and suffering were embedded in the habitus to construct a hegemonic masculinity through a range of practices at the school. This is a common theme in the construction of masculinity through aggressive, combat sports in both Western and non-Western settings.

Furthermore, as in the initiations in our research discussed earlier, ritualised bullying and bodily suffering were all regarded as part and parcel of proving one's worth as a man.

Masculinity was also sometimes tested and proven through harassment and abuse of women (see also Dempster, 2009). Previous research has shown how many men acquire social status and respect from other men through the use of degrading and objectifying language, which establishes the 'ideals, fantasies and desires' of control, dominance, and authority that is associated with hegemonic masculinity (Connell, 2005, 838). The use of sexist and objectifying language and imagery by men students (and staff) functioned as a means of establishing gendered power relations, through degradation and humiliation, and also through potentially threatening behaviour which might have the effect of silencing, intimidating, or even coercing women to 'go along' with it rather than to challenge such practices.

> Later on at the sports ball I went outside for a smoke and they were like, 'hey you're the girl that was sat right behind us on the coach. Oh God you've got great breasts, can I motorboat you [putting one's face between a woman's breasts and a turning one's head rapidly from side to side while making a noise like a motorboat]?' And I'm stood there with four of the lads round me and I'm like, I don't know what to say so I let them do it to me.
>
> (Naomi, woman, U3)

The silencing impact of laddish behaviours is significant for understanding how such practices can continue to be so widespread in university environments. Humiliation, intimidation, and violence are used to establish a hierarchy and to control and silence victims of these

What Does Lad Culture Look like?   45

practices. The salience of gendered power relations renders it difficult for women to challenge such practices without fear of retribution or reprisal – physical or otherwise. Participants noted how men staff, as well as students, engaged in sexist banter, language, and behaviour, thus reinforcing the sense that such behaviour is acceptable and normalising it as part of the culture of that department or institution (this is discussed fully later in this chapter). As Page and Whitley (2015) note, the power that occurs in staff-student relationships, specifically, renders it difficult for students to name and reject these misogynistic practices. They note that there are particular social and institutional mechanisms that 'enable, circulate and conceal sexism' (Page and Whitley, 2015, 35) and that make the work of 'seeing' and challenging sexism and harassment in universities difficult. Phipps and Young (2015a) have also noted that sexism and sexual harassment may be deliberately concealed by universities in a bid to 'preserve marketability in a neoliberal context' (Phipps and Young, 2015a, 305).

Other Ways of Othering

Although lad culture was most closely associated with sexism and misogyny, most participants also spoke about the ways in which lad culture crossed lines of gender, sexuality, ethnicity, social class, and dis/ability:

> If there's a group of lads, they give each other nicknames as a kind of a jokey thing, you know. Some of the nicknames we've heard are things like paedo, gay boy and token black as examples of some of the nicknames I've heard of people with. And then they go round town on a social, write it on their shirts as if they're wearing it as a kind of trophy kind of thing, and they're proud to have that nickname.
>
> (Naomi, woman, U3)

> We had another case of a student with Asperger's actually, who was bullied on social networks, on Facebook but didn't have the self awareness or enough social awareness to realise that he was being bullied. And the nature of the bullying was very sexually explicit, calling him names, mocking him because he didn't have girlfriends or he was acting weird around girls.
>
> (Sam, woman, U4)

> So for example, while I was at [name of university where she was employed previously], there was regular for example graffiti on white boards in classrooms which was, you know, homophobic, sexist, those kind of things. And very much done because it's part of lad culture, having a laugh, ha ha way.
>
> (Jessica, woman, U2)

46   *What Does Lad Culture Look like?*

Thus, lads also targeted Other men, men identified as Other by their difference from the white, middle class, heterosexual norm. This finding is salient for extending our conceptualisation of laddism from being about gendered power relations in isolation, to highlighting its entanglements with other systems of hierarchy and oppression. In Chapter 3 we return to sport with a particular focus in that chapter on the intersections between lad culture, sport, and social class. Now we turn to homophobia and racism.

Homophobia and Racism

Homophobia was identified as a core feature of lad culture by many participants in our study. Homophobia was deployed as a tactic of humiliation and dehumanisation of the Other, defined against the normative, heterosexual white man.

> I think it quite often includes racism and homophobia and disableism and kind of just criticising and dehumanising everything that differs from the white, straight, able-bodied man norm that usually plays sport kind of thing.
>
> (Kate, woman, U6)

> I've seen things like homophobia. I should point out at this point that I am gay. I've seen homophobia in and around groups that I would define as being part of that lad culture.
>
> (Jeff, man, U4)

> I think it ties in with expectations of men and women and the banter that surrounds that, because the whole idea [is] of a camp man being less of a man, I suppose.
>
> (Alex, woman, U4)

Homophobia was manifested in a range of forms, including banter, themed parties (e.g. 'drag socials'), and homophobic graffiti in teaching rooms. Homophobia was not strongly associated with any particular group of people, although men's sports teams were mentioned on numerous occasions as being involved in homophobic chanting and using homophobic language. Sports culture more generally was perceived to be exclusionary and marginalising through its establishment of straight, white, cis masculinity[1] as characterising the idealised and normative lad.

> Here in U5, to be a gay man and try and participate in the lad culture is very difficult. It often means you have to suppress your, I don't necessarily mean be closeted, because you can be openly gay.

What Does Lad Culture Look like? 47

But you'd need to suppress certain elements in order to fully participate in the lad culture.

(John, man, focus group, U5)

Anderson, McCormack, and Lee (2011) have argued that sporting initiations are now more focused on alcohol consumption than on homophobic activities as a vehicle for demonstrating hegemonic masculinity. In
what they argue is a time of decreasing homophobia and homohysteria,
they note that same-sex activities traditionally used during initiation rituals no longer symbolise the threat to heteronormative masculinity that
they used to. However, our data suggest that homophobic language and
practices were used by sports teams (and others) to establish and reinforce the desired and ideal embodiment of (heterosexual) masculinity
(see also Jeffries, 2019). Homophobia sometimes intersected with racism and other forms of discrimination in its function to degrade and
establish social and cultural power over Others, and the two featured
simultaneously in some participants' narratives about lad culture. Staff
narratives thus suggested that homophobia and racism co-existed as part
of lad culture in university.

I suppose the pejorative side of lad culture is the one that we certainly see reflected in the newspapers and it's very clearly about a
culture which may be explicitly or implicitly sexist, homophobic,
sometimes racist.

(Elsa, woman, U2)

It's an attitude of banter, it can be sexist, homophobic and racist and
it generally comes from group activities in a certain setting, and it's
quite binary of what it is to be a man and what it is to be a woman.

(Alex, woman, U4)

Specific examples of racist behaviour were less frequently mentioned,
but the forms that racism most often took were chanting, jokes, and
banter. Phipps and Young (NUS, 2013) note that in their study racism
was often presented as 'fun' or joking, for example, by white students
'blacking up' for birthday or other celebrations. Our data show similar
patterns of racist behaviour. A number of staff either minimised racism
by suggesting that perpetrators were 'unaware' of the implications of
their behaviour, or took the view that racism was no longer deemed acceptable and therefore was not a significant part of laddish behaviour: 'I
think race features as part of that but I think it's more racism out of ignorance and naivety' (Phil, man, U5). The notion that laddish behaviour
can be attributed to naivety and that lads are not really racist or sexist is
picked up in Chapter 4 where we explore participants' explanations for
laddism. In this chapter we now consider banter in more depth.

Banter

> I think it's [the term lad culture] generally used to signify, it's gangs of lads. It's what's euphemistically termed banter. Very often associated around either watching or playing sport I think. Very much a drinking culture ... seen as quite confrontational, quite dismissive of other groups outside of the lads.
>
> (Josh, man, U3)

> So swearing, loud, banter, taking the piss out of each other, totally inappropriate non-pc statements which no-one seems to mind, and just general sort of very much laddy ... not anti-women but quite sexist in a sense.
>
> (Lucy, woman, U2)

'Banter' was a frequently listed constituent of lad culture. Many of the behaviours described by staff narrating lad culture centred on particular performances of masculinity and related to establishing power, control, and dominance over other men and/or women. Phipps (2017) has noted that laddish behaviours may be used by middle-class young men to humiliate those identified as Other, including their working-class counterparts. We note that consideration of the ways in which students' experiences of harassment and violence are cross cut by multiple and intersecting characteristics is vital: gender, sexuality, ethnicity, social class, dis/ability, and age are significant to being identified as Other to the white, male, cis, heterosexual, and middle-class norm. Banter, chanting, humiliation, intimidation, objectification, and violence were means through which such gendered power relations were achieved and sustained; we explore these more fully in Chapter 4 when we discuss explanations for laddism, but we introduce them here as they constitute key ways through which laddism was performed.

There is very little academic research on banter specifically, including the ways it is deployed to humiliate, intimidate, or degrade. However, as Phipps and Young (NUS, 2013) note, banter can be used to disguise sexist, homophobic, and racist values by framing such attitudes in the discourse of a 'joke' and shaming those who feel offended. Our participants recounted numerous examples of witnessing banter in university settings.

> And you know, I feel theoretically there should be nothing wrong with having a banter over football or what you did last night in the pub. And on the face of it there isn't. But because that masks other more sinister kinds of positioning of women, and jokes about women, and jokes about women's rights and all that kind of stuff, that's why it's problematic I think, because it serves that function.
>
> (Heather, woman, U6)

What Does Lad Culture Look like? 49

One of our sabbatical officers said she stood up to give a speech, you know at the student elections, and there were male students whistling her. And I was stunned, shocked by that. Because I thought, you know, I just imagined that had gone, that sort of behaviour. But she was saying, no it's prevalent across the site, that generation, almost a sort of post-ironic sort of approach. And I was just so shocked that that was there.

(Jack, man, U6)

Our participants noted the ways in which sexism, harassment, and abuse were often downplayed, trivialised, or invisibilised through banter (see also Chapter 4). Its discursive form and function as a 'joke' makes it difficult to call out the sexism contained within banter. Sexism – as a structural form of discrimination – is re-narrated as 'just a laugh', an individual attempt to make a joke: 'Like I said, they're sort of harmless. It's not horrible. There's no malice in what they're doing; it's just the fact that they're juvenile, annoying and quite loud' (Lucy, woman, U2). The wider context in which such banter originates and is located, and its function in reinforcing particular gender stereotypes and dismissive or degrading attitudes towards women, in particular, is rendered invisible. Through the use of banter, those at the receiving end of discrimination, harassment, or abuse can be positioned as problematic, as complaining, as taking 'a joke' too seriously. As Whitely and Page (2015) note, anger in response to sexual harassment or abuse can sometimes be reinterpreted as bitterness, especially if the cause of the anger is dismissed or goes unrecognised. Drawing on Campbell's (1994, 50) work on power relations in emotional responses, they note, '[f]or a charge of bitterness to be issued there must be a "collaboration of a certain mode of expression (recounting of injury) with a certain mode of response (failure to listen)"' (p 37). We extend this conceptualisation of dismissal to the use of banter to dismiss and trivialise sexism, harassment, and violence; the recipient of sexism or harassment is positioned as 'bitter' because of the collaboration between the mode of expression (banter) with an expected response (laughter). The victim-survivor's 'failure' to respond appropriately and their discursive positioning as 'less than' – as the brunt of the joke – allow for a dismissal of their emotional response. Ahmed (2010) has also argued that in the context of survivors' voices being heard in response to sexual harassment or violence, they are positioned as 'complaining', as 'feminist killjoys' who have exposed bad feelings. This symbolic and discursive ostracisation of survivors renders banter a powerful means of invisibilising, and thus of sustaining, sexism, harassment, and violence.

And it's all wrapped up with this idea of it just being a laugh and it's not serious and it's all a joke. Which is actually really, I think, a

50 *What Does Lad Culture Look like?*

clever defence for any criticism of it because it immediately allows those people involved in the lad culture to say 'oh you don't get it, we're just having a laugh, it's not serious'. And I think that jokey element is really important to that lad culture.

(Jessica, woman, U2)

The gendered, classed, and racialised hierarchy which could position sexism, racism, homophobia, or classism as 'funny' was often left unspoken, thereby reinforcing the normative and hegemonic positioning of those (mainly men) using banter. Only some of our participants recognised the implicit hierarchy assumed by, and reinforced by, the culture of banter.

I suppose it depends on your definition doesn't it, but I suppose banter might be harmless to some people but if you're the subject of the banter as opposed to producing it then you may not see it in that way. And of course who knows what that then leads on to.

(Diana, woman, U4)

Most people who are participating in lad culture are performing it for each other and so in that sense it's aimed primarily at other men. And that would, I assume, make people with other sexual orientations, for example, very uncomfortable. So I think it would disadvantage people with different sexual orientations.

(Lisa, woman, U4)

High-profile media stories of university students engaging in misogynistic and racist chanting have noted how this is an increasingly pervasive feature of lad culture in university settings (e.g. BBC News, 13 October 2014). Cheeseman (2014) has discussed the ways in which chanting is used in the same way as banter to ridicule, humiliate, or degrade students. As we discuss more in Chapter 4, chants frequently draw on themes of classism, sexism, and violence against women to discursively establish superiority or dominance. Our data similarly suggest that chanting by groups of students – often, but not always, sports teams – features sexual violence, physical assault, classism (often framed in terms of university rivalry), and homophobia. This was a discursive vehicle for enacting misogyny and harassment, and was sometimes accompanied by physical abuse too:

So, I mean my friend once told me that when she was in her first year - which was probably about 4 years ago - the rugby team were having a social in our bar. They pulled her up onto a table and chanted around her and then called her a slag and stuff and then pulled her down again. She really hated that.

(Alex, woman, U4)

What Does Lad Culture Look like?   51

Both chanting and banter were varyingly viewed as not seriously intended, as reflecting young people having fun, as being naïve about how their behaviour might be viewed, and as not intended to cause harm.

> So it can be homophobic, it can be sexist, but I don't think it's vindictively so, it's not maliciously so. It's seen as banter by the people that are doing it. And they would be mortified if they ever thought for a second that somebody thought they were intentionally going out to be homophobic or sexist. But he's gay so we'll sing a song about that and he's a bit fat so we'll sing a song about that and he's got a beard so we'll sing a song. You know, it's not seen as anything other than that.
>
> (Josh, man, U3)

This depoliticised view of the reasons *why* students engage in banter and chanting – which we pick up again in Chapter 4 when we discuss explanations for laddism – reveals the ways in which particular vehicles for sexual harassment and violence can trivialise and invisibilise its impact on other students. Banter was also used by staff in teaching and learning contexts, and it is to these contexts that we now turn.

Lad Culture in Teaching and Learning Spaces

Despite the predominant representation in the media and in previous research of lad culture as a phenomenon involving sexual harassment and abuse in *social spaces*, our participants narrated many examples of gender-based harassment in teaching and learning spaces too. These ranged from disruptive behaviour – such as frequent interruptions or refusals to engage with whole-group discussions – to sexist interventions, including sexist comments in response to tutor questions, on end-of-module evaluation forms, and degrading comments towards fellow (women) students. Understanding more fully the range of ways in which lad culture permeates university contexts enables an analysis of the less overt and more insidious ways in which sexism and gender-based harassment and abuse manifest in higher education. It also allows us to conceptualise lad culture more broadly, thinking about it as operating beyond 'extreme', highly visible examples of misogynistic harassment and violence. This has implications for how prevalent lad culture is perceived to be in higher education settings.

Laddish Staff

> I had a fairly shocking instance of it from a senior lecturer, who I think must be in his 50s, a couple of weeks ago. [He] made a really inappropriate comment. He was the only man in the room, people

52   *What Does Lad Culture Look like?*

filtering in for a meeting. He happened to be the only man, he'd arrived early and a group of women walked in and he said, 'oh, I've got a harem'.

(Elsa, woman, U2)

The role of the university in perpetuating sexist attitudes and behaviour extended to practices aimed at women staff as well as at women students. Some staff members explicitly identified laddism as encompassing a lack of respect towards women lecturers and women students, and suggested that this was reinforced – in some instances – by men academics too (see also Jackson, Dempster and Pollard, 2014). They gave examples of the ways in which male staff members colluded with male students to create an environment that was intimidating for women students: 'Last year a male science lecturer set up a picture of a half-naked woman on his lecture slide saying "there's something for the lads to look at during a lecture", which got quite a lot of complaints' (Kate, woman, U6). Women lecturers were also subjected to sexist remarks and disruptions in teaching and learning spaces (as discussed later in this chapter) by students as well as by male colleagues. This was more common in some disciplines than others, and was particularly frequent in 'masculine' areas such as sports science and business and management. The culture of the academy was described as 'Not straight lad culture but boys' club culture which is almost like the grown-up version of it' (Kim, woman, U1), and as marginalising along gender lines even when sexism was not the focus of practices being discussed. For example, a number of women participants talked about men in their institutions using football as a topic of conversation to create camaraderie among each other, as well as with men students.

I mean certainly even with staff in our department, they'll exchange banter about football and all that kind of stuff. But obviously none of it kind of relates to, you know, they're not talking about women or kind of positioning that against women … But, you know, they'll talk about football and they'll share banter about football and they'll kind of, do things that I would see as laddish that I can't be part of that conversation. So I think that happens but I mean it's not severely discriminatory in any way.

(Heather, woman, U6)

While this type of banter did not explicitly draw on sexism or misogyny it was still perceived as having a marginalising or excluding effect on those constructed as unable to participate, mostly women. The use of football as a subject of conversation was viewed as reflective and productive of a particular form of masculine performance, as 'using the tools of lad culture' (Jessica, woman, U2) to establish gendered boundaries

What Does Lad Culture Look like? 53

of inclusion and exclusion. Paula Burkinshaw (2015) argues that such performances serve similar purposes in higher education senior leadership teams. Through her in-depth exploration of how women vice chancellors negotiate and navigate higher education leadership cultures, she argues persuasively that university leadership teams are communities of practice of masculinities of which women, even women vice chancellors, can never be full members. The sports banter acts as a bond in that community for many, while excluding others. As one of her women leaders contends:

> When you are group of leaders together leading a university there's a fair amount of banter and social stuff that's going on and that's severely gendered, endless football and cricket discussions, partly I'm not interested in sport but they are male sports I can't imagine them getting excited about women's hockey or something, there's a lot of being comfortable with each other that's to do with gender, that's not leadership but it's part of bonding as a team that maybe you have to find ways that you can interact with them on a social level, to make the leadership bit work well rather than make yourself always look slightly odd.
>
> (Burkinshaw, 2015, 86)

Our participants talked about the ways in which banter was also used by staff members to generate a sense of 'camaraderie' with students: 'when he talks about trade wars with China he will use the example of bras because that gets laughs from the classroom' (Katrin, woman, U4). This was narrated as a specifically gendered tactic, used primarily by male staff members to engage male students. This is a pattern that has also been identified in schools. Jackson's (2010) work in secondary schools in England illustrated that many of the men teachers in her research engaged in laddish banter in their classrooms to (attempt to) gain the respect of the lads and establish classroom control. She argues that while such strategies are appealing from an individual male teacher's perspective, they are, nevertheless, highly problematic for several reasons:

> First, such laddish displays may fail to engage, or earn the respect of, non-laddish boys and girls, and so their learning and enjoyment may be impaired. Second, from feminist perspectives laddish behaviours are problematic as they reinforce sexist and often homophobic versions of masculinity. Third, laddish teachers can make life more difficult for colleagues who will not, or cannot, be laddish. As a result, rather than working together teachers may be working against each other, with some attempting to reduce laddish behaviours at the same time as others are (sometimes apparently inadvertently) reinforcing them.
>
> (Jackson, 2010, 516)

54   *What Does Lad Culture Look like?*

This critique is also applicable to higher education. The use of banter by staff working in universities contributes to the institutionalisation of sexism, where its 'perpetuation [is] bound up in the structures of the institution' itself (Whitely and Page, 2015, 38). Furthermore, its simultaneous openness and yet concealment through individual and organisational practices renders it nigh on impossible to challenge.

> Lad culture makes it difficult for female staff to challenge because it belittles sexism. Social media additionally trivialises laddish behaviour; male staff may even use social media to perpetuate running 'inside' jokes during subject sessions on teaching and learning.
>
> (Kim, woman, U1)

Laddish Students

Although lad culture was more likely overall to be associated with social spaces, this varied between institutions according to student demographics and the physical estate of the universities. Lad culture tended to be identified as an issue in *social spaces* more often when institutions recruited predominantly 'traditional' students who lived on or close to the university and where there was a vibrant social scene locally. It was presented as less of an issue in social spaces in institutions where students were predominantly 'non-traditional': this descriptor covered a range of characteristics, including Black and minority ethnic (BME) students, mature students, students with caring responsibilities, and local students. The 'non-traditional' make-up of the student population was associated with lower levels of laddish behaviour as these students were perceived by staff not to engage in typical student nightlife and drinking cultures due to their family responsibilities, living away from the university, religious beliefs, or cultural differences.

> But a lot of our students live at home ... they're mature, they have families, they have placements, they don't act like traditional undergraduate 18-year-old students.
>
> (Sandra woman, U1)

> I don't know if you've see round, there is a Students' Union and there is a bar but a lot of our students don't drink, they live at home, they're older. So in terms of the night time economy, I don't think [name of university] contributes a great deal.
>
> (Sue, woman, U2)

In institutions where there were predominantly 'non-traditional' students, lad culture was more often seen to be an issue in teaching/learning contexts (especially in U2), whereas this was far less commonly referred to in the institutions with a predominantly 'traditional' student demographic (universities 4–6). However, there were a few instances of classroom lad culture in pre-1992 institutions, and our data seem to reflect Phipps' (2017a) observation that there are differences in the forms of classroom laddism between elite and non-elite universities. Phipps (2017a, 822) argues that 'when laddish masculinities have been reported in the classrooms of more elite universities, these have tended to be characterised by a more domineering demeanour which has been defined as intimidating to women, rather than disruptive'. We argue that the distinction between these forms is not clear-cut and there is considerable overlap between them; nevertheless, there are hints of this distinction in our data. A common theme throughout participants' discourses around laddism in teaching/learning spaces was the notion that this type of behaviour was levelled primarily at women lecturers, thus underscoring the gendered basis for such harassment and abuse. The example below is one of very few examples of direct, visible classroom laddism from one of our elite universities:

> A colleague of mine was giving an interactive lecture on India and she said 'does anyone know how many women are in the Lok Sabha parliament?' - one of the houses of parliament - and there was a cry from the back from somebody of 'too many' … You encounter this. I certainly, in my department, I encounter a lot of misogyny and these sort of jokes about feminism, about women, about all these sorts of things. It's really prevalent.
>
> (Paul, man, focus group, U5)

There were also distinctions in terms of the directness or the visibility of such instances. A less visible form – in terms of it not being public and the student's identity being hidden – was via anonymous student evaluations of women staff. For example, Pete (U2) told us about a lecturer who had been described as 'MILF' [Mother I'd like to fuck] on a feedback form.

The types of classroom laddism that involved disruptive behaviour or refusal to engage with academic work in lectures were reported as more common in the post-1992 institutions. Behaviour descriptors, which parallel the ways laddism has been described in school contexts, included coming to class without having prepared to participate or contribute to academic discussion, frequent interruptions to the lecture/lecturer, heckling or undermining the lecturer or other students in the session: 'He would come into a lecture or a teaching session late on a consistent basis, he would eat, talk, burp, laddish I think behaviours' (Pete, man, U2). As well as being more frequently reported in post-1992 universities, it was also reported to be more common in some disciplines than others, most notably in management schools and sports-related areas, both of which are highly 'masculine' domains (see also Jackson et al., 2015). For example:

56   *What Does Lad Culture Look like?*

For sports programmes in particular, this can be problematic for staff. Male students can be disruptive in lectures and male staff don't help because they tolerate those behaviours or don't challenge these behaviours. When female and/or mature students challenge it, it is turned around on them instead of placing the responsibility on the male 'offenders'.

(Karen, woman, U1)

In Chapter 4 we return to laddism in teaching and learning contexts, when we discuss possible explanations for it. At this point we want to note that our findings suggest that lad culture in higher education should be considered beyond its forms and impacts in social spaces. Understanding the varied and in some cases subtle ways in which lad culture permeates higher education contexts allows us to think about the settings in which sexism operates in more insidious, less overt ways. A unilateral association of laddish behaviour with alcohol consumption and particular sports teams may mean that other forms of sexism and misogyny go unrecognised or become normalised, and that its impacts become harder to monitor and tackle. Indeed, the perception of staff overall that lad culture is not particularly widespread in higher education but that it is confined to particular contexts and (groups of) individuals supports this. It is to this issue that we now turn.

Perceptions about Prevalence: The In/visibility of Lad Culture

We don't notice it, so I think it's quite accepted. Because when I was first thinking about lad culture at this university I thought 'oh well there isn't really' and then I realised actually there is and there's quite a lot of it. It's something that even I sometimes don't even notice.

(Alex, woman, U4)

Throughout this chapter we have explored what our interviewees perceived lad culture to be and the spaces they associated with it. In this final section we critically explore perceptions about its prevalence and pervasiveness. In particular, we explore, explain, and refute the notion proposed by a sizable proportion of our interviewees that lad culture is not widespread within their institutions.

The institutionalised invisibility of lad culture referred to by SU Officer Alex earlier may be explained in various ways. One possibility is that lad culture is not an issue in higher education contexts, or at least not a widespread one. However, previous research (see Chapter 1) and our analyses in this project cast considerable doubt on the validity of this explanation. Rather, like Alex, we argue that it is widespread but much of it is rendered invisible for numerous interrelated main reasons.

What Does Lad Culture Look like? 57

First, as discussed earlier in this chapter, many of our interviewees' understandings of laddism corresponded to the limited conceptualisation of lad culture depicted in the UK media. In the press lad culture is portrayed as involving highly visible performances of hegemonic masculinity including excessive alcohol consumption and 'extreme' examples of sexual harassment. Similarly, for many of our interviewees lad culture was portrayed as 'extreme' and perpetrated in isolated incidents by a handful of problematic individuals, rather than as a pervasive culture that produces, reinforces, and normalises gender-based harassment and violence in a range of forms.

> Yes, [lad culture is] certainly evident, we've certainly had disciplinaries; I think people being abusive of women ... male students, not people, male students being abusive of women staff here. Shouting like on a building site with students driving around here shouting at female students; two or three incidents of female students being accosted. Reporting at the Student Union that the atmosphere could be quite intimidating and harassing in there. So it's definitely here. I wouldn't say for a moment that it's predominant in any way ... I've had female students come and report unwanted attention or assaults or non-consensual, but I've never had the feeling this was a massive problem or there were dozens of these cases. And I also quite strongly have the feeling that it's very much disapproved of by the vast majority of the students, male and female. So I think it certainly exists but I don't think it predominates.
>
> (William, man, U4)

> I suppose [there are instances of laddism] once or twice a year that I'm aware of. I wouldn't say it's endemic and I wouldn't say it happens all the time, but there are certain times of the year - at the end of the academic year, large sporting events - where it's more likely to happen.
>
> (Tom, man, U5)

Thus, the pervasive 'everyday' instances of sexual harassment and violence, or what Lewis et al. (2018, 67) refer to as 'the "wallpaper" of sexism', were rendered invisible.

Second, and closely related, only high-profile, extreme cases received staff attention and action:

> By the time the issues come to me, then I'd say it's [laddism] fairly infrequent but I can imagine that if I investigate it I'd probably find that it's a lot more frequent than it appears ... I think if I really stuck my nose in, then I probably would find that there's a lot more instances occurring than actually come to my door. Normally by the time it comes to my door, it can be pretty serious.
>
> (Ella, woman, U2)

58   *What Does Lad Culture Look like?*

Ella is not alone in not 'sticking her nose in' to find more instances; as Sundaram (2018) has argued, university agendas to produce critical global citizens who seek to challenge social inequalities such as sexual harassment and violence come into tension with the reality of increasingly individualised, neoliberal modes of teaching, assessing, and interacting with students. Indeed, in the context of creeping marketisation of higher education where institutional reputation is essential for ensuring high market value, it is not in a university's interests to look for, or even encourage students to report, cases that may result in adverse publicity. As Towl and Walker (2019, 1) argue, 'Sexual violence thrives under a veil of (open) secrecy. And knowingly or otherwise, as university communities we have colluded with this either implicitly or explicitly'. While reputational damage was not a major theme in our interviews (we did not ask about this directly), it emerged in a few instances. For example, while we were discussing an institution's and individual's willingness to take part in our project, William (man, U4) opined:

> If anything comes out, everybody says 'well, I'm not sure we should be washing even the tiniest bit of dirty linen in public' ... I think we should wash dirty linen in public on the grounds that dirty linen exists everywhere to a certain extent and it's better washed really. We obviously shouldn't over-publicise it; we certainly don't want it to seem that because we are willing to address it we've got a problem with it.

In stark contrast with 'washing dirty linen in public', the steady marketisation of higher education has produced university contexts that often seek to silence or erase any threats to their marketability. As Phipps (2017b, 358) argues, 'for something to be marketable it must be unblemished: everything must be airbrushed out'. Thus, in an increasingly neo-liberal context, lad cultures, sexism, and sexual harassment in higher education may be invisibilised by institutions to preserve their market value and standing (Phipps and Young, 2015a). Interestingly, several high-status universities declined an invitation to be involved in our research, in some cases explicitly citing concerns about reputational risk as the reason.

Third, partly because of the limited conceptualisation of lad culture among many of our participants, there was a notion that it was evident largely or exclusively in social spaces, especially venues that sold alcohol. Thus, there was a common perception that lad culture was not visible to them because they did not frequent spaces in which laddish practices occurred: 'I have a sense that it's probably quite bad like that but because I don't see it, I don't know it' (Sophie, woman, U3). Indeed, as we discussed earlier, those staff who did frequent student social spaces – mostly SU staff – reported lad culture to be rife. We also provided a lengthy

What Does Lad Culture Look like? 59

example from Abby, noting that the ubiquity of sexual harassment is, ironically, one of the reasons she cites for not highlighting or reporting it. It is so commonplace that it is normalised. Thus, its ubiquity and normalisation is another reason for its invisibility; it is not made visible to higher education institutions by students through complaints processes. Barriers to reporting also include, as Abby and other research suggests, a lack of clarity about channels for reporting and concerns about how reports will be handled (Alldred and Phipps, 2018). Furthermore, even when reporting occurred, a lack of joined-up information sharing and gathering within the institutions meant that there was no holistic picture. Some of our interviewees conveyed this with a sense of frustration:

> Interviewer: Do you think that lad culture is an issue in the university?
> All I can say, I don't know. I was going to say I'm limited in the fact that what I deal with, I deal with any issues that are causing concerns for students in university accommodation. What issues there are out there in the clubs and pubs and things like that, and in the Students' Union and in general - I'm probably not the authority to ask about that. When we deal with things within university halls, we just deal with them on what the incident is about, so it's about noise or is it about bullying, is it about sexual harassment, is it sexual assault? We get very few of those [sexual assaults] but we do get some.
>
> (Tony, man, U3)

UUK (2016) has also highlighted and condemned a lack of systematic recording of instances of lad culture at institutional level, which prevents not only the development of a holistic picture but also of a whole-institution response.

Overall, the lack of recognition of the prevalence of lad culture, sexism, and sexual harassment presents an obstacle to institutional work to challenge such practices; its relative invisibility to staff renders the need for challenge and prevention invisible as well. As Sara Ahmed (2016) has written, when sexual harassment becomes invisible, so too does the labour of trying to challenge it. We return to the challenges in Chapter 5.

Summary

In this chapter, we analysed the ways in which university staff encounter lad culture and delineated the underlying elements of laddish behaviour, as well as the contexts in which it is experienced and the ways in which it is 'hidden'. We demonstrated how sexism and misogyny are central to lad culture, and highlighted the ways these intersect with homophobia and racism. Our analysis also exposes the insidious ways that sexism operates within university contexts, mediating teaching and learning

60 *What Does Lad Culture Look like?*

encounters, as well as social situations. It also demonstrates the complicity of institutions in perpetrating and perpetuating lad culture, at the level of individuals as well as organisational cultures. Sexism is experienced as institutionalised and therefore as difficult to challenge for staff and students alike. In the following chapters we analyse in detail who is perceived to engage with lad culture, and why.

Note

1 While we characterise the idealised 'man' as straight, white, and cis, we did not have many examples of transphobia in our data. We know that transphobic harassment and abuse do occur in universities (for example, Rivers, 2015), but no examples of this were narrated to us by university staff in this study.

3 'They're Mainly Private School, White Boys'
Who Are the Lads?

Introduction

In the previous chapter we introduced and discussed how our interviewees perceive lad culture and explored their narratives about where and how it is manifest. In this chapter we take these initial explorations further as we analyse staff views on who engages in lad culture, examining the intersections between gender, social class, ethnicity, and age, as well as the spaces and contexts that are perceived to cultivate it. Understanding who is perceived as laddish and in what ways is crucial if we are to theorise lad culture which, as Phipps points (2017a) out, remains under-theorised and requires an intersectional approach. The chapter is structured around key social categories that interviewees used to describe and define who is laddish. Lad culture was very strongly associated with men and masculinities, so we start by discussing gender, exploring the ways in which women and men are positioned in discourses about lad culture. We then move to consider the ways in which staff perceived lad culture to be related to social class, age, and ethnicity. We realise these social categories intersect, but separate them in this chapter for the sake of clarity, while also highlighting the intersections.

Gender

> We don't really think it's just lads … it's big groups of girls as well, sometimes.
>
> (Isabelle, woman, focus group, U1)

As discussed in Chapter 1, in line with most of the previous research on laddism, we conceptualise it as a particular way of 'doing gender'. While people of all genders can perform 'laddism', it is very strongly associated with men and masculinities, both in this and previous studies. Furthermore, it has been argued to be closely associated with hegemonic masculinity – a culturally exalted, high status, dominant form of masculinity – in numerous contexts including schools and universities

62 *Who Are the Lads?*

(Frosh, Phoenix and Pattman, 2001; Younger and Warrington, 2005; Jackson, 2006a; Dempster, 2009, 2011; Jackson and Dempster, 2009). For these reasons, our discussions in this book about laddish performances relate almost exclusively to men and masculinities, and discussions about women relate predominantly to the effects of lad culture on them. However, in this section we explore how laddish women were constructed and perceived by our interviewees, and how gender informs the ways in which laddish performances were read, judged, and understood.

In our project laddism was most strongly, but not exclusively, associated with men: some women were also regarded as being laddish, or 'ladettes'. The dominant view among our sample may be summed up as: women can be laddish but there are more laddish men than women; men are laddish more frequently; men perform more forms of laddism, and more extreme forms, than women. Aspects of this view were voiced by Will: 'I don't think it's equal between men and women, I think it's far more men, but I do think there are women who do engage in it' (Will, man, U5). Thus, there were generally seen to be quantitative (more men are laddish and more often, and men perform more forms of laddism) and qualitative (men are more extreme) differences between men's and women's performances of laddism. In this section we explore and analyse these differences. We argue that despite men overall typically being regarded as quantitatively and qualitatively *more* laddish, close analysis of comments suggests that laddish women are often judged relatively more harshly and portrayed more negatively than their men counterparts.

As we argued in Chapter 2, laddism among men was associated with a range of practices, including sexism, misogyny, homophobia, racism, sexual harassment, and violence, and frequently associated with contexts where alcohol consumption took place and/or sport was a focus. However, among women, laddism was associated with a very limited range of practices and contexts; it was almost exclusively associated with alcohol consumption and to a lesser extent sport, both of which have strong and long-standing associations with masculinity (Dempster, 2009, 2011; Lebreton et al., 2017). The most pernicious core aspects of men's lad culture – sexism, misogyny, sexual harassment, and violence – were not seen to feature in women's lad culture (we return to this point later).

Laddism among women was perceived to be increasing, which interviewees attributed to increases in women's alcohol consumption leading to rowdiness (see also Jackson, 2006b).

> And it's not just within lads anymore, you can definitely see it within females - the lad culture growing - especially from being in a sporting background, that's where it stems from with females. And I think it's just growing now into people or into girls that don't even necessarily

Who Are the Lads? 63

take part in sport but take part in the lad culture: in drinking and rowdiness and being a bit over the top.

(Karen, woman, focus group, U1)

Interviewees' narratives about laddish drinking cultures among women invariably entailed women being judged negatively and often more harshly than men. In some instances, concerns about women's health and welfare were embedded in the critique.

I think the lad culture behaviour has been there all the while. I think probably the most difference while I've been here is probably because the involvement of women has been more - nowhere near the same amount as males - but there have been noticeably issues around consumption of alcohol and what that's produced ... Women have been found half-naked on stairs, absolutely, completely out of it; where there's been issues of alleged sexual assault and it's been difficult to get information because the females don't remember.

(Tony, man, U3)

Tony conveys concern for women's safety, but there are hints of victim-blaming in his narrative. Here and in popular discourse women are judged and held responsible for being sexually assaulted if they have been drinking. By contrast, although evidence suggests that alcohol consumption among men is associated with higher levels of sexual assault, men are not judged more harshly for perpetrating sexual assault while drunk (Jensen and Hunt, 2019). Indeed, as we explore in Chapter 4, drunkenness is often presented as a reason to judge men's laddish behaviours *less* harshly.

Excessive alcohol consumption is also a defining feature of the way that ladettes have been constructed and portrayed in the UK media, and such portrayals are almost invariably extremely negative (Jackson and Tinkler, 2007). As in Tony's narrative above, some of the disapproval expressed by the press about women's drunken behaviours is couched in discourses relating to concerns about their health and wellbeing. However, based on an extensive analysis of media representations of ladettes, Jackson and Tinkler (2007) argue that concerns about women's health and wellbeing cannot account for the extremely negative portrayals of them. Rather, they argue that it is the way that ladettes transgress gender boundaries and challenge the traditional gender order that explains their vilification. Ladettes are presented as 'aping men' and as 'displaying behaviours and attitudes that transgress normative femininity and so are criticised for being "too masculine"' (p. 262).

Discourses about laddish women transgressing normative femininity and 'aping' men were also strong in our research, and women were

64   *Who Are the Lads?*

invariably criticised for such behaviours. For example, Grace (U4) refers to her shock at women fighting 'in the same way that boys used to', even though she has not witnessed such events herself: 'to be fair I'm slightly out of touch, I just hear stories':

> That's [excessive alcohol consumption] a huge social problem we've had for years here but it seems to have got a lot worse hasn't it. And I think the shocking thing is that it's acceptable. I mean I'm an old fart really [laughs] but you see girls and the state they get themselves into, and fighting in the same way that boys used to. It's really shocking to see it ... I think it's the female students that have changed their behaviour, I don't think male students have changed particularly.
>
> (Grace, woman, U4)

Grace's narrative reflects two interrelated dominant discourses about young women: that they are aping men's behaviour in order to claim equality, and that equality is now firmly established as women's drinking is acceptable among young people. Both of these discourses are challenged by researchers. For example, Bailey et al.'s (2015) interviews with middle- and working-class young women (19–24 years old, including groups of undergraduate students) suggest that excessive drinking is not acceptable for women: it is regarded as unfeminine, and the 'wrong look' (see also Lebreton et al., 2017). Indeed, the spectre of the 'drunken slag' – a reviled figure with which none of the young women wanted to be associated – was omnipresent throughout their interviews (see also Skeggs, 1997, 2001, 2004). Moreover, Bailey et al.'s women undergraduate interviewees were particularly keen to disassociate themselves from what they presented as the 'drunken immoral figure of the "chav"' who is associated with the 'unrespectable' working class (p. 753; see also Tyler, 2008). However, paradoxically, drinking is marketed as part of a 'good night out' for women, and also as a sign of empowerment, autonomy, and 'sassy' contemporary femininity (p. 748). Thus, Bailey et al. convey the complex ways in which young women must negotiate celebratory discourses about drinking, hedonism, empowerment, and autonomy, and contradictory derisive discourses that associate extreme drunkenness with a loss of respectability (see also Marsh, 2018; Jensen and Hunt, 2019).

Such tensions and negotiations are not evident for men. Heavy drinking is regarded as a marker, and expectation, of hegemonic masculinity, and although there are expectations that 'real men' are able to hold their drink (Dempster, 2011; Lebreton et al., 2017), getting drunk is still acceptable. Indeed, as Dempster revealed based on his study of laddism in one pre-1992 university in England, being awarded 'Piss-head of the Year' was worn as a badge of pride by men, whereas such

Who Are the Lads? 65

an award had negative implications for women. The double-standards about men's and women's drunkenness were made explicit by one of his interviewees:

> Females who do drink a lot ... that's a turn off. I think the worst thing to see is either your girlfriend or someone female you know absolute legless ... But for males it's seen as a more acceptable thing ... Males are perceived to drink more and perceived to handle more and ... the sort of prehistoric culture ... the cavemen would say, 'we are the men, you women are our objects'.
>
> (Dempster, 2011, 642)

Thus, evidence suggests that contrary to Grace's (U4) assumption and also popular discourse, drinking to excess is not acceptable for women in the same way that it is for men: gender double-standards remain strongly entrenched. The continued existence of these gendered double-standards, and the sanctions that women face when they transgress normative femininity, cast doubt on the notion that women are trying to 'ape' men when they drink or play sport. Yet, women are frequently castigated both for trying to meet 'male standards' and for failing to meet them. This reinforces the notion of the 'male as norm' and of women striving and failing to be 'as good' as men (Jackson and Tinkler, 2007). The idea that women are trying to copy or ape men was a recurring theme voiced by those interviewees who argued that women are laddish.

> But also I think there are some female students that can display quite laddish behaviour. They kind of get into similar crowds and are you know, aping the behaviour of the lads that they're with, participating in all of the activities that I've just explained to you ... some female students ape that male behaviour, sort of ladette, laddish culture and engaging in binge drinking, you know, chanting, that kind of thing. But by no means as bad as some of the stuff that comes up with the lads.
>
> (Hannah, woman, U6)

> I did have to deal with students who, more like the laddism I was talking about earlier, where the girls were trying to be like the boys by drinking pints and being ill the next day. I had those kind of things where they were trying to prove they were the same, you know going out and breaking an arm playing rugby or whatever.
>
> (Lauren, woman, U2)

> I think there is an element of that as well that women have started to, I don't know, be a bit more like men, you know to be able to fit in. That sometimes their interpretation of equality is to adopt the

66   *Who Are the Lads?*

bad behaviour that they've maybe seen by other males within their social circle.

(Barbara, woman, U1)

Contrary to these assertions, an enormous body of research suggests that rather than women acting 'a bit more like men ... to fit in', most women work hard to perform normative models of femininity in order to be accepted. This is especially important if women are entering into domains or performing behaviours typically associated with masculinity (including drinking and sport), as they have to work even harder to 'recoup' femininity which may be 'lost' or questioned by them doing so (Holland, 2004). This work is particularly acute for working-class women whose respectability is always more precarious than for their middle-class counterparts, as dominant discourses position working-class women as excessive (drinking, smoking, sex), disruptive, crude, and aggressive (Skeggs, 1997, 2004; Jackson and Tinkler, 2007). So most women students have to negotiate contradictory discourses on nights out. On the one hand drinking is a marker of fun, autonomous student life in UK universities. On the other hand, drunkenness is regarded as unfeminine, unrespectable, and undesirable. Or as Bailey et al. (2015, 754) put it: 'The performance of hypersexual femininity was constructed as a necessity, although excessive drunkenness was seen as unfeminine and viewed as damaging their ability to perform the "right" form of femininity'. As such, far from attempting to ape or be like men, most young women are attempting to negotiate the contradictory demands of performing the 'right' form of hyperfemininity and an 'optimum' level of drunkenness (Bailey et al., 2015, 755).

Such contradictory demands were largely absent in portrayals of laddish women undergraduates in our interviews, which is perhaps not surprising as they are also absent in popular discourse more broadly. The dominance of postfeminist discourses in which girls and women are seen as 'having it all' and being able to 'do it all' (Harris, 2004, Ringrose, 2012) renders invisible the many gender inequalities and double-standards. Indeed, such postfeminist discourses often cast girls and women as the winners at the expense of men (Gill, 2016). Certainly there was some evidence of this in our research. For example, Jeff cast women's sports teams' behaviours as the same as, or more extreme than, men's:

The kind of ladette group which I very much see as the netball girls or the hockey girls or whoever they might be were just behaving quite funnily in a more extreme way than their male counterparts. As a kind of group, big drinking, big dancing, big flirting, quite obviously objectifying men in exactly the same way.

(Jeff, man, U4)

Others cast men as being penalised by the notion of lad culture:

> Other welfare officers thought that lad culture was just penalising men and actually it should be called lad and ladette culture. It should have a different name because what it is isn't about men's behaviour as a group, which is I think what everyone thinks of straight away, but it's about an attitude that we all have.
>
> (Alex, woman, U4)

Some even suggested that lad culture is not a problem relative to ladette culture:

> The Education Officer at the Students' Union has claimed there is 'no problem' with lad culture but more of a problem with 'ladette' culture.
>
> (Kim, woman, U1)

Although such views were minority views, they warrant our attention. In particular, they are worthy of consideration and scrutiny because they reflect a broader tendency evident among many of our interviewees to judge laddish women relatively more harshly than their men counterparts. The term relatively is important here. As we have already noted, most interviewees – although not all – regarded men as qualitatively and quantitatively more laddish than women. However, women seemed to be judged disproportionately harshly given that laddism among women was almost never seen to include sexism, homophobia, racism, sexual harassment, and violence – the most pernicious aspects of laddism among men: 'you don't get a group of women together out drinking who make homophobic slurs in the way you do with what I perceive to be those groups of men that embody the lad culture' (John, man, focus group, U5). The important differences between men's and women's laddism were rarely acknowledged and discussed. The cases below provide important exceptions.

> Interviewer: Would you see it [lad culture] always being or involving men?
>
> I think primarily yeah ... I think women could maybe be involved but it would be in a different way and it would make you feel different, I think. I think also you're less threatened by women doing similar sort of behaviours ... I think you're less likely to experience any kind of actual harassment or physical abuse by women. So when men are kind of perpetuating this culture around you, it's tied in with your expectations that you might actually have to deal with the effects of it targeted at you.
>
> (Chloe, woman, U6)

68 *Who Are the Lads?*

Some went even further when prompted, and noted that women's laddish behaviours, rather than making other people vulnerable, were more likely to make the woman herself vulnerable.

> I just think young women do different stupid things, but they do stupid things.
>
> Interviewer: Are those stupid things things that harm other people...?
>
> No I don't think so, and I think they harm the individuals [women] more as well ... like the drinking culture and how young girls are making themselves more vulnerable to predator attacks and things like that.
>
> (Ruth, woman, U1)

Chloe (U6) and Ruth (U1) are relatively unusual as they offer the beginnings of a gendered analysis of laddish men and women. Harassment, sexual assault, and violence against men by women are rare; the vast majority is against women by men (see Chapter 1). Chloe's account acknowledges this difference, and that threats from groups of rowdy women and men are not the same, and are not felt in the same way. This is in stark contrast to the gender-blind approach of Jeff (U4) when he suggests that women are 'quite obviously objectifying men in exactly the same way [as men do women]' (see also Gill, 2016). To suggest they are 'exactly the same' ignores decades of work by feminist scholars which highlights the ways in which women's bodies are routinely objectified in ways that men's are not (e.g. Bordo, 2004). It ignores the ways in which the objectification of women's bodies is located within a patriarchal system. It ignores gendered power differences and intersections between sexuality, ethnicity, social class, dis/ability, and age. It ignores evidence that the vast majority of sexual harassment and assault is perpetrated by men against women.

We are not denying that harassment of men by women does not occur, but it is rare. In our research we encountered one example. Interestingly, while we were told countless stories of women not reporting harassment, and/or their reports being ignored; the case involving a man being harassed was addressed immediately:

> A male student came to a security guard at some point last year and said that three or four times in a row, even though he'd asked her to stop, a girl kept grabbing his crotch. And the result of that on the night was to ask her to leave, so she had to leave the premises.
>
> (Jim, man, U4)

We do not want to overstate the attention given to 'laddish' women in this research. As noted, most staff associated laddism primarily with men.

Who Are the Lads? 69

Furthermore, almost all staff suggested that laddism was more prevalent, frequent, and extreme among men than women. However, it is very important to analyse the ways in which women were portrayed when they were discussed, and to unpack and analyse the gendered assumptions underpinning the comments. Our analyses suggest that laddism is performed very differently by women and men; the impacts on others also differ. That laddish women were sometimes judged more harshly than laddish men does not reflect the behaviours of women and the impacts of them on others, rather it reflects the ubiquity of pernicious gender double-standards. While laddish behaviour by men was seen to include sexism, misogyny, sexual harassment, and violence, none of these were regarded as evident in women's lad culture. Yet despite these most extreme and deleterious elements being absent for women, laddish women were still judged severely.

Social Class

I would see it as more of a class thing: so a working-class culture. But of course that's not true. Actually lad culture is very present amongst upper-class men ... but we don't call it lad culture ... So I think that lad culture is many things, but for a long time I only really associated it with working-class culture ... My examples are from the late '70s ... now it seems not to be restricted to a particular class.

(Sue, woman, U2)

Sue's comments reflect the changing associations of lad culture with social class from the 1970s to the present. These associations are delineated in our Introduction to the book, so we provide only a brief reminder here. In the 1970s being 'one of the lads' was strongly associated with working-class white boys and young men. For example, Paul Willis (1977) applied the term 'lad' to a group of white, working-class, anti-school boys in his classic study *Learning to Labour*. The association between white working-class boys, academic 'underachievement', and laddism is still evident in policy discourse, and was especially strong during the height of the 'moral panic' about boys' so-called 'underachievement' in secondary schools in the late 1990s and early 2000s (Epstein et al., 1998). A significant body of research in the late 1990s and 2000s disputed the assumed connection between laddism, social class, and underachievement by providing evidence that middle-class high achieving boys are often laddish too (Jackson, 2006a; Francis, Skelton and Read, 2010, 2012). Nevertheless, associations between disruptive classroom practices, working-class boys/men, and laddism remain, both in secondary school and higher education contexts (Jackson, Dempster and Pollard, 2015). We start by reminding readers of the associations

70 *Who Are the Lads?*

between social class and laddism in teaching/learning contexts discussed in Chapter 2, before moving on to focus on social spaces.

As we discussed in Chapter 2, lad culture was more often seen to be an issue in teaching/learning contexts in our post-1992 institutions (especially in U2) where there were predominantly 'non-traditional' students, whereas this was far less commonly referred to in pre-1992 institutions which had a predominantly 'traditional' (middle-class) student demographic (universities 4–6). We noted that in the post-1992 institutions classroom laddism was characterised in similar ways to how it has been described in secondary schools, notably, as involving disruptive behaviour in class and/or refusal to engage with academic work: coming to class without having prepared to participate or contribute to academic discussion; constant interruptions to the lecture/lecturer; heckling or undermining the lecturer or other students in the session. As well as being more frequently reported in post-1992 universities, it was also reported to be more common in some disciplines than others, most notably in sports-related areas and management schools (see also Jackson, Dempster and Pollard, 2015). We pick up discussion of lad culture in teaching/learning contexts in the next chapter when we discuss explanations for laddism. Now, we turn to laddism outside of the university classroom, which was much more frequently discussed, and where the class-associations seem markedly different. As Phipps (2018a, 174–175) argues:

> in contrast to the mainly lower-middle and working-class framing of classroom disruption, the sexist "lad culture" which has been identified recently in the social and sexual spheres of university life appears to be largely (although not exclusively) the preserve of privileged men.

This very much accords with our data: outside of university teaching/learning contexts, laddism was most commonly associated with middle-class or privileged (white) men.

> When I think of kind of lad culture, I tend to think, not so much of working-class people, I think people who are maybe from a little bit more privileged backgrounds … I think that would be the group that I would associate that kind of culture with. You know, you think a little bit like the Hooray Henrys, that kind of thing. But not even at that level, probably a bit more middle class where there's a little bit more money about.
>
> (Barbara, woman, U1)

> So what I would say for [University 5] is that the laddish behaviour is in that upper [class] group, not in the lower [class] group, okay. So I don't see laddish behaviour being manifested by some of the more,

Who Are the Lads? 71

by some of the WP [widening participation] population, by the BME [Black and minority ethnic] population amongst the students.

(Nancy, woman, U5)

I've seen it most, being most dominant and most prevalent, in the institutions I've worked in that have been dominated by middle-class white men, both as staff and as students.

(Jessica, woman, U2)

It's a bit of a sweeping generalisation as with lots of these things, but quite often white upper-class students ... the kind of Bullingdon Club[1] sort of mentality.

(Marion, woman, U4)

Although laddism was most commonly associated with middle-class or upper-class (white) men, this does not mean that our interviewees did not identify and talk about associations between lad culture and working-class boys and men. Many reflected critically on the ways in which lad culture is identified, inflected, and in some cases labelled differently, depending on whether it is performed by working-class or middle-class men.

I think lad culture is probably inflected slightly differently according to social class. And certainly in terms of how it expresses itself is quite encoded for social class. But I don't think it belongs to a social class. So the kind of stereotyped white British working-class lad heavily invested in football and a pub culture is no more a lad than the middle-class teenager out on the lash in Ibiza really.

(Elsa, woman, U2)

Martha (U2) had checked the dictionary definition of lad culture before our interview, and noted and also challenged the association with the working classes:

When I read the definition in the dictionary, I'm still not quite sure of the relevance of it, because it defined laddism or laddish behaviour as sort of loutish or kind of sort of drinking culture, working-class or sort of lower-class if you like, and sort of bullying and loud. And I was thinking, I'm sure that's not really what you're really asking me about ... You sort of think of it as a class thing where at least certainly in the dictionary it suggested it was a class thing, which I thought was quite interesting. But actually I've been in quite a lot of environments where you would say that very wealthy, privileged people have very very similar behaviour, boorish and kind of over the top. So it's certainly not a class thing.

(Martha, woman, U2)

72   *Who Are the Lads?*

Like Martha, Jack (U6) also acknowledged dominant discourses that link lad culture with working-class people, and notes the class-specific ways that the lad-culture label is applied.

> [Lad culture is] what people see as a young working-class male culture which is drinking and football ... I've always found that it's often used in relation to, you know, young working-class girls are called ladettes often in the media, and it's often used when people talk about Maguluf and places like that ... I've always felt that there's a sort of a working-class element to it when people talk about that. And you know when you see Oxford and Cambridge students misbehaving, when they're leaping off bridges naked, people don't call it a lad culture.
>
> (Jack, man, U6)

Jack alludes to the class-specific double-standards at play when judging and labelling laddish behaviour, which were identified far more frequently than the gender double-standards discussed earlier. Some of our other interviewees highlighted in stronger terms the ways in which similar behaviours were cast differently according to whether the actors were read as middle/upper- or working-class. For example, Paul (man, focus group, U5) stated vehemently that 'When poor people do it, it's anti-social behaviour!' Rebecca (U4) made a similar point, but rather than referring to how behaviours are read differently by a generic audience, she refers specifically to students' own 'snobbish' perceptions of themselves and each other. In Rebecca's narrative below, the choir boys' high levels of cultural capital are exemplified through their displays of high culture and elite taste (Bourdieu, 1984), and contrasted with their neighbours' popular culture, poor taste, and undesirable friends.

> And there's the choir boys who think it's fine because they can make a noise, but if they're drinking brandy in a gown and they're playing an instrument then it doesn't matter because it's actually educational, and they're bantering about it, and it's their view about what's acceptable. And they have a very snobbish view that that should be allowed because of what they're talking about and what they're drinking. Whereas somebody next door, if they're playing rap music and maybe smoking out the window and their friends aren't as desirable, they're in the wrong. They're just, they're quite, I find a lot of students quite judgemental about each other actually.
>
> (Rebecca, woman, U4)

Rebecca alludes to the choir boys assuming that they were immune from trouble because of their high levels of cultural and social capital, what we label as 'entitled immunity'. A strong, class-specific discourse of entitlement was identified by many of our interviewees when discussing

Who Are the Lads? 73

laddish men: interviewees narrated the ways that middle- and upper-class men did not expect their laddish actions to lead to deleterious consequences; they were reluctant to accept responsibility or accountability, and if necessary, they would get their parents to 'bail them out'.

> There's this kind of narcissistic temperament that they think, whatever they get up to, mummy and daddy will bail them out of it.
>
> (Barbara, woman, U1)

> The really bad incidents we've had there has been a lot of privilege in the students who were there ... we've had two incidents where the groups have got really really drunk and trashed once a bedroom, once a kitchen and it was, talking to the guys who trashed the kitchen, I got the sense that they seemed stunned that this was even an issue that they had to be accountable for. Well, unfortunately it is! There is an element of they're used to doing what they want but also not having it challenged by anybody.
>
> (Sally, woman, U5)

> So some of the ones that have come here are a little bit disconnected from society because society's become disconnected from them. The ones at Cambridge were disconnected because their daddy would pay for it. So when it went wrong and the punt had sunk with people on board, daddy would take care of it or daddy's lawyer would take care of it.
>
> (Ruth, woman, U1)

> Going back to this public school thing, there's a certain extent to which they're more reckless because they have no problem in rectifying those mistakes if they need to.
>
> (Paul, man, focus group, U5)

The discourse of entitlement will be picked up again and discussed in the next chapter. It is worth noting here though that Rebecca's follow-up comments, reported at length below, suggest that the privileged students do tend to be treated more leniently than less privileged students who 'don't play the game' and so are perceived to be 'asking for it'.

> And then you've got some of the rugby, boarding school boys who can be just as poorly behaved but in some ways seem to charm their way through it, rather than the ones who'll be a bit more louty I suppose ... There's definitely a clear sign between those who come in here: 'I've done wrong, I know I've done wrong but I'm going to charm my way out of it, I'm going to play the game, I'm going to be oh yeah but we're just young and we're just growing up, when we were at boarding school we did this and it's no harm'. ... I think

74 *Who Are the Lads?*

generally as an institution, those who've got a boarding school background and are a bit of a charmer blatantly get away with far more. Because also I think there's an element of, if you're doing well academically, it's all part and parcel, that's the main thing ... I think well actually, look at how much they're disturbing everybody else and just because they've managed to maybe sit in front of a disciplinary committee, they're well dressed, they come from a good background, they've managed to charm their way out of it, their father's a lawyer, they've maybe got a scholarship, they went to a good school, it's oh they've made a mistake, we'll move on. And I just think it's quite natural, you get somebody there who maybe, we've had students who've maybe got criminal records or they maybe just don't present themselves in the same way, don't help themselves, they don't play the game. They'll sit there defensive: 'well what's your problem, why should I do this?' and people then just think well, OK you're asking for it.

(Rebecca, woman, U4)

Although Rebecca is in some ways critical of the system in which privileged students are more likely to be treated more leniently than less privileged students, she nevertheless presents the latter in deficit terms: they don't help themselves, they are too defensive, they don't play the game. This assumes that they know what the game is, know how to play it, and want to. Yet as Diane Reay's (2017) work illustrates, universities, and particularly elite universities, represent middle- and upper-class worlds in which working-class students are always 'outsiders on the inside' (Reay, 2017, p. 151). Many working-class students do not know what the game is, or how to play it (Bathmaker et al., 2016). In some cases, they may not feel entitled to play it, or may not think that it is morally appropriate to do so (Abrahams, 2017).

The strong association between middle/upper-class men and laddism in universities extended into sporting contexts. As we discuss in the next section, laddism was strongly associated with sports teams and sporting contexts, and particularly with rugby union which is largely the preserve of middle-class, white, privately educated men (Collins, 2009).

Social Class and Sport

The rugby club: I think their captain was dismissed this year because they went on a drunken rampage through [city] smashing up clubs and student residencies and doing things like, I don't know, going to the toilet outside residences and getting blood everywhere and kind of like extreme vandalising. And that involved the rugby club there and that was quite a big story.

(Chloe, woman, U6)

As we discussed in Chapter 2, there is a very strong association between lad culture and sporting contexts (Jackson 2006a; Dempster, 2009; Nichols, 2018; Jeffries, 2019), and this was certainly evident in our research. The majority of our interviewees commented on the association:

> Not exclusively sports teams, but I find in my experience it's been intrinsically linked to sport.
>
> (Josh, man, U3)

> I think it's more likely to be done by young men involved in sport (Alex, woman, U4).

> It's often associated with types of societies like football clubs and other sports clubs.
>
> (Karen, woman, U3)

> It's again a lot of your usual suspects, the football team, the rugby team, they all go out in packs, you'll never see one of them on their own.
>
> (Stephanie, woman, U3)

> The rugby club or the football club.
>
> (Heather, woman, U6)

In Dempster's (2009) research on laddism among men in a pre-1992 university in England, university sportsmen were identified as exemplars of laddishness, and men's sports teams as the primary sites for the construction and performance of laddish masculinities. Furthermore, there was a hierarchy of sports and, in line with the earlier comments of our interviewees, rugby and football topped the laddism table, both in terms of the number of laddish players and the extremity of their actions. In Dempster's research, 23 out of 24 (96%) of his undergraduate interviewees identified men rugby players as typical lads, and football players were labelled as laddish by 21 of the 24 (88%). As noted previously, laddism is not one thing, but rather is a constellation. Dempster's interviewees portrayed men undergraduates as on a continuum with 'proper lads' at one end and 'non lads' at the other end. The 'proper' lads were typified as the 'rugby boys' and were seen to perform the more extreme forms of laddism (see also Jeffries, 2019). This continuum was evident in our research too, with the majority of our interviewees associating laddism, especially the more extreme forms, with sport teams, and especially men's rugby (see also Nichols, 2016). Indeed, almost all accounts of the more extreme forms of laddism involved men's rugby teams. Furthermore, as we illustrate below, laddism was particularly strongly associated with rugby union.

In his detailed social history of English rugby union, Tony Collins (2009) demonstrates how 'rugger boys' – because of their 'willingness to

76 *Who Are the Lads?*

give and take violence' and because the game is built on 'the assertion of masculinity through physicality' – were and still are regarded as the epitome of manliness (p. 74). His fascinating analysis through the 1800s to the present day illustrates how deeply rugby union is part of the privileged, middle- and upper-class world of private education. He charts the ways in which rugby union is built upon misogyny, class privilege and entitlement, and Imperialism. Furthermore, he discusses, as we did in the last chapter, the ways in which being a rugby (union) player is about much more than the game – it 'sought to forge masculinity' through entry to an elite club that required commitment on and off the pitch:

> once accepted into membership [often after a gruelling initiation ceremony] heavy drinking was expected of the new recruit. Simply playing the game was not the done thing ... Behaviour off the field, as well as on it, built a player's reputation in the eyes of his team-mates.
>
> (Collins, 2009, 86–87)

Thus, the strong associations between rugby and laddism are not surprising; the intersections of laddism, rugby and white, middle/upper-class, entitled masculinity were writ large in many interviewees' accounts.

One particularly notable and lengthy account was conveyed to us by Kate, a member of Student Union (SU) staff at University 6. Kate's seemingly well-rehearsed, clearly articulated account of a very traumatic incident suggested that she has spoken about it many times, which she confirmed during our conversation. It also echoes similar occurrences at other universities (for example, Stirling) that have been reported in the press (for example, *Huffington Post*, 20/11/2013). Kate told us:

> I was on the bus with a few friends going out for the night and we were at the top of the bus near the back, and then I think a few stops on the whole of the University of [name] rugby team came on in their post-match suits and everything and were obviously quite drunk and there were about 40 of them and they came up being all rowdy and drunk and stuff. And I think they first asked me and my friends to move so that they could have the back area of the bus ... and we were like 'no, we're sitting here' kind of thing and so they all kind of filled up in front of us, probably about 10 rows of seats where they were sitting, standing all in the alleyways kind of being really loud and stuff and after a while they started chanting and singing a song called Chicago which I hadn't heard before ... some of the verses are horrendous ... most of them are about sexual assault and then there's one verse which is almost at the end and instead of the sexual assault it was, a woman she came into a store, an orgasm she wanted, who gives a fuck what she got. So it's actually showing

Who Are the Lads? 77

just the degrading of women when they do actually have sexuality as well as kind of saying, they're just there for men to get their sexual fill. So it was really really offensive and there was also some racial slurs in there as well, it refers to a girl from Indo China who had rice in her vagina I think was one of the things. ... I basically got into a bit of an argument with the captain on the bus, asking him to tell his team mates to stop and explaining why it was so offensive and all this kind of stuff and we had a bit of an argument and he was quite loud and aggressive and just unpleasant ... and then when they got off the bus I think there was some kind of initiation or something. They said the first years had to go out the window, so this is the back window on the top of a double-decker bus when the bus stopped, and they asked us to move so they could make these first years jump out of the window quite drunk and we were like 'no' and they were like, climb over, so there was like two guys who managed to climb over us where we were sitting or standing to jump out the back of a window of a bus quite drunk onto a road where there was traffic. So I mean there's quite a lot in that situation that kind of speaks for lad culture and the hierarchy within that as well and the captain refusing to do anything about it.

Later in the interview, Kate returned to her discussion of laddism and rugby, but this time her comments were couched in terms of social class and privilege.

I think actually when you look at like kind of public school private school white boys, there is definitely a different kind of lad culture that's much more, I don't know, the kind of rugbyesque lad culture that you see chanting and all gathering together and all that kind of stuff.

She noted that her encounter on the bus was with the rugby *union* team, and when narrating her experiences of working with various sports teams after the bus incident, she reflects on the intersections between sport, social class, and entitlement discussed earlier:

Rugby Union is like a kind of more public school, southern version of the game and much more rich. Whereas the Rugby League [team] is much more working class, like they don't have suits and they were the group who were much more open to listening and changing and didn't want to perpetuate their stereotypes ... I think maybe the working-class groups of men are much more like, it's maybe not having come across opposition to stuff like that before and [they] wouldn't necessarily want to perpetuate those discriminations. Whereas I think maybe the more middle-class public-school

78   *Who Are the Lads?*

lad culture is much more educated: I know what I'm doing and I don't care and I'm going to do it anyway.

Kate, like interviewees quoted in the previous section, conveys a strong sense of entitlement among middle/upper-class, public-school educated men, and contrasts this with her experiences of less-privileged men who are members of the rugby league team. Here then, we get more insights into intersections of laddism, sport, and social class.

The most common tropes of laddism were all evident in Kate's account, namely: men's sports teams (in this case combined with initiations), alcohol, loud boorish behaviour, and sexism (see also Warin and Dempster, 2007). It is also a particularly striking and visible instance of lad culture and, as we discussed in Chapter 2, perceptions about the extent and seriousness of lad culture were strongly influenced by their visibility (see Jackson and Sundaram, 2018). At another institution an incident was particularly high profile because the target of the rugby club's abuse was a senior member of staff:

> Something happened with one of the rugby teams, I can't remember which one it is ... so they were shouting abuse at [the close colleague of a very senior member of the University] - of all people to shout something at! And she was pregnant and they pretty much shouted at her that they wanted to pin her down and rape her.
>
> (Sophie, woman, U3)

The shouting and chanting also increased the visibility, and again was particularly associated with sports teams:

> I went to our sports ball and throughout the whole entire journey of the bus I was sat at the back next to the rugby team, and also the netball team were there, which was a group of females. And for the whole entire journey the rugby lads were doing lots of chants and those chants were very much focused on sexualised behaviour. They had one song which was a call and repeat song which involved picking out one of the netball girls and identifying her by what colour dress she was wearing and linking that with a sexual act that she 'liked to do'.
>
> (Naomi, woman, U3)

We return to many of these issues in the next chapter when we discuss explanations for laddism. Now though, we turn to laddism, ethnicity, and age.

Ethnicity and Age

> It does seem to be young white males, young white British males.
>
> (Rob, man, U3)

Who Are the Lads? 79

Rob's comment reflects a strong majority view among our interviewees that the vast majority of lads were young, white British men. Some interviewees commented that Continental European men could be laddish occasionally, as could North Americans and sometimes British-Asian men.

> I would suggest that it's much more likely to be performed by home students. To a certain extent EU students as well, but definitely to a lesser extent. International students much less likely.
>
> (Jim, man, U4)

> But also here we find that we have quite a lot of young Asian males, and so British-Asian males who do behave in this way as well.
>
> (Marion, woman, U4)

Once again, intersections were noted with privilege. For example, Rebecca (U4) comments on the wealth of two laddish French students, as well as Asian students:

> We've had a couple of French students the past year who will do what they want when they want ... they've offered to bribe security not to give their names out. And they are what I class as high-end laddish behaviour. They think it's funny, they've got a lot of money, they're all in designer clothes. And they'll have parties late at night and they'll hide people in their showers, under their beds when security comes round and they think it's funny ... Last year it was more of an Asian group of guys, very, had plenty of money.
>
> (Rebecca, woman, U4)

Interestingly, Chinese students were singled out and marked as not being laddish:

> We have a lot of international students from countries like China. I don't think they get involved at all. But I do think that [students from] some other countries do, some other European countries.
>
> (Alex, woman, U4)

> Most of them, all that I'm aware of, are those instances really which would all be mainly white males ... You almost never get any Chinese students, ever. Most international students, you very rarely get any of them involved in those kind of behaviours.
>
> (Tony, man, U3)

Our finding that Chinese students were marked as not laddish echoes that of Francis and Archer (2005). Francis and Archer explored British-Chinese secondary school pupils' constructions of laddism, and found that (mainly non-Chinese) teachers suggested that British-Chinese boys

80   *Who Are the Lads?*

were never laddish, whereas a substantial majority of pupils thought that some do behave in laddish ways. There are important differences between their research and ours. First, they were researching secondary schooling rather than higher education. Second, their work focused on British-Chinese students, whereas the references in our earlier quotations are to Chinese students studying at an English university. However, key aspects of their research are of relevance to ours. Francis and Archer note that Chinese students are generally constructed as serious, hardworking, responsible, focused on education, and conformist, and that these constructions tend to be associated with femininity in the United Kingdom, and thus are positioned in binary opposition to laddism. The dominance of such constructions meant that staff in their research were less likely to read the behaviours of British-Chinese students as laddish; instead they tended to homogenise British-Chinese students and see them as diligent, high-achieving, 'good' pupils. While we have insufficient data about Chinese students to draw any conclusions, the very limited available data are in line with Francis and Archer's findings and analyses. For example, one of our interviewees, Mei (U5), who is Chinese, suggested that some Chinese students were laddish at university, and that laddism is also an issue in China.

JOHN: Is there any lad culture in the Chinese community?

MEI: I think so, I think so, but it's just a few, because I'm on duty for the post-graduate students and I've found out they normally drink at home and just are not too drunk. ... [they] have a proper dinner and chat, rather than just get drunk.

INTERVIEWER: Is it an age thing because they're slightly older?

MEI: Yeah, yeah, they know what they want to do and they're past the age. Like they [already] did the same thing as undergraduates, so they grow up, they don't need to do it again ... But in China we've got something like this as well. It's really big news. In [the] newspaper we saw a really serious case like with several superstars, and then they got really naked pictures everywhere in the newspaper, Facebook, Chinese Facebook, everywhere.

So why might Chinese students be singled out as not laddish by everyone except Chinese staff? Francis and Archer's conclusions noted earlier are likely to be applicable. Relatedly, research on visibility and intergroup relations may offer insights. Such research suggests that people tend to regard 'outgroups' (groups to which they do not belong) as more homogenous and less interesting than their 'ingroups' (groups to which they belong), and this is exacerbated when outgroups are perceived as less powerful than the ingroup (Sherriff, 2007; Jackson and Sherriff, 2013). Jackson's research in schools, for example, illustrated how boys tended to homogenise girls. Furthermore, most boys displayed remarkable ignorance about girls' lives as their focus was almost entirely on themselves

Who Are the Lads? 81

and other boys. Sherriff's (2007) analysis, based on his research in a secondary school, led to similar conclusions. His research revealed that dominant laddish boys homogenised lower-status, outgroup members (who included girls), and were generally unable to speak about what outgroup members did or how they spent their time. In general, dominant boys assumed that girls actually did very little, and certainly nothing of interest. In many ways what girls (and 'lower-status' boys) did was completely invisible to the boys, and particularly the 'popular' boys. Jackson and Dempster (2009) also highlighted a similar pattern among higher education students. Thus, as we argued in Chapter 2, there are a range of factors that shape the in/visibility of lad culture and affect staff perceptions about who is laddish, where laddism is evident, and how prevalent it is.

In relation to our findings, it is possible that as almost all of our interviewees were white British they would have been more likely to homogenise Chinese students and draw on stereotypes. It is important to note that we are not suggesting that there are high levels of laddism among European Union (EU), overseas students, or British students from minority ethnic communities. However, it is also important not to homogenise and stereotype students. It would be naïve and dangerous to assume, for example, that there is no sexual harassment or gender-based violence among Chinese students. Indeed, reports about Chinese women students fighting against sexual harassment in Chinese universities have gained increasing prominence on social media. One example is a piece published in the *South China Morning Post* (16/01/2018) under the headline: 'Chinese students use #MeToo to take fight against sexual harassment to elite universities: Activists say petitions calling for more action on abuse and discrimination have been filed at up to 50 top colleges in past week alone'. Thus, we need to be attuned to the ways that ethnicity intersects with other social categories in the construction of lad culture and, as Phipps (2017a) argues, to theorise laddism differently depending on who is performing it.

Mei brought age into the discussion about laddism among Chinese students, noting that postgraduates (with whom she works) are less likely to be laddish because they are older and have 'been there and done it'. We now turn to considerations of age.

Age

The vast majority of interviewees associated laddism with young men rather than with 'mature' students.

> I think broadly speaking it's, you can't really pigeonhole a particular group, other than you can probably categorise it by age: it's the 18-to-24-year-old bracket.
>
> (Tom, man, U5)

82 *Who Are the Lads?*

It's definitely 18 to young 20s. The older the students are the less likely you'll see these behaviours in them. But that may be because of the different places they socialise and also the possibility that actually they don't socialise on our campus at all, but commute from further afield. It's that classic age group of young white males 17 to 25.

(Jim, man, U4)

Not only was laddism associated with younger men, but it was presented as more acceptable among younger men: laddism among older men was referred to as 'weird' and 'sad' (which implies it is not 'weird' or 'sad' when performed by young men).

Oh yes, I suppose age comes into it, yes: young, and I would say before 30 I think, talking of lad culture after 30 would seem weird to me.

(Sam, woman, U4)

Lad culture is specific to young people and the way it is expressed is specific to young people. When older men do it, it's a bit sad and it looks different and is regarded differently.

(Sandra, woman, U1)

Nichols (2018, 75) argues that the association between age and laddism is linked to both the 'boys will be boys' narrative and life course perspectives. She argues:

Within both the narratives of laddism and "boys being boys", there is the underlying assumption that the behaviours and interactive practices associated with young men, including laddism and associated ideologies, are temporary, and so laddism is understood to be tied up to particular moments of the life course.

However, Nichols argues that laddism remained a prominent feature in the lives of the men in her research, who were members of a rugby union club in the north east of England, aged 18–40 years old. She argues that men re/negotiate laddish identities throughout different stages of their lives, and that we need to theorise laddism in ways that avoids presenting lads as static, monolithic characters.

While the vast majority of our interviewees associated laddism principally with young men, and arguably gave young men more leeway than their older counterparts, a minority suggested that laddism is not age-specific:

But I think it's very apparent to me that although the term lad implies a degree of youth, actually we'll see lad culture embodied in the

Who Are the Lads? 83

lifestyles and choices of men in their 30s, 40s, and 50s, not just in teenage boys and men in their 20s.

(Elsa, woman, U2)

That laddism is not confined to young men is evident when we analyse what our interviewees said about laddism among staff.

Staff

Do we have any lads on the staff? I'm sure we have some. Mostly, I would say from what I've seen, it's kind of, there's quite a lot of sexism.

(Diana, woman, U4)

We discussed laddism among staff in some depth in the previous chapter, so we mainly offer a brief reminder here. Laddism among staff was equated with sexism, and always associated with men. Examples related to work contexts – lectures and meetings – rather than social contexts:

I was at a workshop last Friday, I wasn't facilitating it but I was a participant and our Professor of Education, he was talking about the key words which are important when you're submitting a paper and you want to grab attention. So playing it a bit for laughs, or so he thought, he said 'pornography, put in pornography'. So my response to him was - and I really rate him as a colleague and as an academic - but language has meaning and I think for me lad behaviour is a lack of awareness of the impact of language and you know, there's nothing funny about pornography necessarily … And a business lecturer who will do that whole thing about 'guys what you need to understand about women is' and I said, 'look I know you're Australian but you've got to stop', kind of, 'you know I find this really problematic'.

(Sue, woman, U2)

We provided more examples in the previous chapter of instances of sexism by individual men, and these were the dominant forms noted among staff. However, there were also some examples cited of lad culture among groups of staff:

Certainly within the department I currently work in, there's a very strong lad culture that is led by a core group of five or six men who have been in the department for a very long time and are very dominant and very much use the kind of tools of lad culture - the booze, the joking around, sport, the banter - as their modus operandi within the department.

(Jessica, woman, U2)

84 *Who Are the Lads?*

Although laddism among staff was not the main focus of our research, it was clear that many interviewees thought that (men) staff could be and sometimes are laddish (see Chapter 2).

Summary

In this chapter we have posed the question: what social categories of students do staff think are laddish? A considerable degree of consensus emerged. First, laddism is associated primarily with men and masculinities: there are more laddish men than women; men are laddish more frequently; men perform more forms of laddism, and more extreme forms, than women. Our analyses suggest that laddism is performed very differently by women and men; the impacts on others also differ. Laddish women were sometimes judged more harshly than laddish men, but we argued that this does not reflect the behaviours of women and the impacts of them on others; rather it reflects the ubiquity of pernicious gender double-standards. While laddish behaviour by men was seen to include sexism, misogyny, sexual harassment, and violence, none of these were regarded as evident in women's lad culture which focused almost exclusively on women and drinking. Yet despite these most extreme and deleterious elements being absent for women, laddish women were still judged severely.

Second, laddism in *social* contexts was seen to be performed by middle- and upper-class young men whose entitled approaches meant they did not expect to be held accountable for their behaviours and relied on their parents to bail them out. Indeed, there were suggestions that such students were less likely to face sanctions as they knew how to play the system. This discourse of what we refer to as entitled immunity seemed to be particularly evident in relation to men's rugby union teams who were seen to epitomise laddism. Laddism in teaching/learning contexts – in the form of disruptions and lack of engagement – was seen to be performed more commonly by 'non-traditional' students.

Third, laddism was strongly associated with young, white, British men. We noted how Chinese students were singled out as *not* being laddish, echoing perceptions of teachers in secondary school research in the United Kingdom. We discussed these perceptions in relation to stereotypes and assumed homogeneity. In the next chapter we explore how staff explain laddism, where we pick up many of the themes identified in this and the preceding chapter.

Note

1 The Bullingdon Club is an elite dining society associated with, although not affiliated to, the University of Oxford. Founded in 1780 as a hunting and cricket club, it soon became better known for its raucous, hard-drinking

dinners and ostentatious displays of wealth. The vast majority of members previously attended Eton, although a few other major public schools are represented. No women are accepted into the society. Membership has always been extremely exclusive, with the handful of new members accepted each year traditionally subjected to "trashing" – the invasion and destruction of their college bedroom by other Bullingdon members. Many male members of the British Government were members, including prime ministers Boris Johnson and David Cameron. It is known for drunken dinners that end in brawls and destruction of property. (www.theweek.co.uk/65410/bullingdon-club-the-secrets-of-oxford-universitys-elite-society).

4 'But They're Not Really like That'
Explanations for Laddism

Introduction

In this chapter we analyse our interviewees' explanations for laddish behaviour. In doing so we seek to understand the ways in which staff working in UK universities theorise, or understand, the causes of lad culture. It is crucial to understand how staff explain lad culture as such explanations shape how these staff and the institutions they represent challenge lad culture; indeed, they even shape whether staff regard it as something that needs addressing at all.

Staff narrated explanations for men's laddism in a variety of ways. In these narratives we again witnessed the conceptual fog that relates to the term lad culture: interviewees did not discuss explicitly explanations for sexual violence, for example. Most explanations for laddism lacked any gendered analysis and instead referred to peer group influences and the need to fit in, (in)authenticity, 'banter', age/maturity, effects of alcohol, and/or the freedom afforded by a university context. Indeed, authenticity is a major theme in the first part of the chapter. Those who mentioned gender either tended to essentialise laddism as 'boys being boys' or, conversely, suggest that 'it's only banter, they don't really mean it'. While somewhat contradictory, both types of explanations served to discursively reduce men's agency and thereby their culpability. We explore these narratives first, focusing on laddism in social spaces. Then we move to consider explanations for laddism in teaching and learning contexts. Finally, we explore gendered analyses relating to power and competition; such analyses were very infrequent and proposed by staff who had professional or personal interests in gender, equality, and diversity.

Fitting In

Many of the narratives about causes of laddism related to the perceived need to 'fit in' at university.

> Sometimes it's to fit in with the boys as well, that you need to behave in a certain way so that you're not seen as prudish or, you know …

particularly around those teenage years or your early 20s, you very much want to fit in and to be accepted within your social group. It's very hard to stand up and say 'I don't want to behave like that'.

(Barbara, woman, U1)

So there's this whole thing that if someone wants to be socially accepted, you follow the behaviour of what's happening, of what they're doing in order to be accepted. And if you're not then that's when they start going 'oh why aren't you chanting with us, are you gay because you don't want to chant about female boobs?' kind of thing.

(Naomi, woman, U3)

I think it's wanting to be part of the crowd, fitting in, it is that kind of wanting to be respected by your peers. And so it's about wanting to have your place in the pack, and if you're a guy or a girl I think that can be quite strong, you know, the drive to fit in ... I think it's that sense of wanting to be seen to be cool and assertive and I think that's the same for men and women really. I think it's wanting to fit in with the crowd.

(Olivia, woman, U3)

Sports teams are an area where it's [lad culture] more prevalent because you have the initiation culture and drinking, but you also have a lot of peer pressure. There's a lot of pressure within sports teams to be one of the lads, be one of the guys and to fit in with what everyone else thinks.

(Will, man, U5)

There is no doubt that 'fitting in' and making friends are very important for university students: research suggests that concerns about being lonely and isolated create considerable anxiety before starting university and during the early days of university life (Dempster, 2007; Marsh, 2018; Read, Burke and Crozier, 2018). Thus, the comments of our interviewees about pressures to fit in are echoed by students themselves in other studies. What the four interviewees quoted earlier do not comment on, however, is why students need to fit into a specifically laddish culture. In other words, why is laddism a dominant culture?

Steve Dempster's (2007) work is helpful in beginning to address this question from students' perspectives. Based on data generated through interviews and questionnaires with men undergraduates in a pre-1992 university in England, Dempster argues that fitting in depends upon 'appropriate' performances of gender (a finding which has emerged repeatedly in research in compulsory education internationally as well as in countless other contexts). In Dempster's work, laddism was regarded as

88 Explanations for Laddism

an appropriate performance of gender for men in university contexts; being laddish was a way for men to prove their (heterosexual) masculinity. This was also evident in our interviews: 'I think it's almost like they have to prove themselves to be an alpha male almost' (Donald, man, U3). As discussed in Chapter 2, core aspects of laddism typify long-standing markers of hegemonic masculinity, for example, sport, heavy drinking, banter, and a denigration of femininity through sexism and homophobia. The heteronormativity of lad culture was raised by Naomi (see the quotation at the start of this section) and many others in our interviews, who highlighted how men run the risk of being perceived as gay and therefore not being accepted if they fail to join in with their peers' objectification of women (chanting about boobs), which is central to laddism. Although Anderson (2010) and his colleagues (Anderson, McCormack and Lee, 2012; McCormack, 2012) suggest that we are witnessing a decrease in homophobia and homohysteria – which matches the views of many of our interviewees – our and other research suggests that although declining, homophobia and homohysteria are still substantial problems in university contexts (Universities UK, 2016). Furthermore, as Clarke (2018, 19) argues, 'although public discourse around same-sex sexuality has in many contexts shifted from overtly homophobic to homotolerant (Røthing, 2008), the heteronormative privileging of heterosexuality and the othering of same-sex sexuality remains intact'. Heterosexuality underpins laddism, and although homophobia was considered to be a less pervasive feature of laddism than sexism, heterosexuality is nevertheless at its core. This was evident in Jeffries' (2019) research which involved interviews with seven, British, white, middle-class, heterosexual men aged 20–21 who were all students in a northern post-92 university in England, and who all identified as 'lads'. His interviewees suggested that racist language was unacceptable but homophobic language was common, although perhaps predictably none of his interviewees saw themselves as homophobic and suggested that it was just 'banter' (this is picked up again later in this chapter). The centrality of heterosexuality and homophobia to lad culture was also evident in Dempster's (2007) work. For example, Andrew, one his interviewees, 'positioned gay men as a group who might encounter a "hard time" being accepted as lads' (p. 185) and spoke about how he did a lot more flirting with women during his early days at university to demonstrate that he was 'not gay or anything' (p. 185) in order to be accepted. Thus, lad cultures act to police men by Othering those who are not, among other things, heterosexual and sexist.

Andrew's reference to the 'early days at university' highlights the way in which work to fit in is more intense and salient at some points than others. The transition to university is one such point. Dempster (2007) argues that his men undergraduate interviewees identified particular

Explanations for Laddism   89

pressures to act laddishly during the transition to university as a way of fitting in; what's more, it was presented as a familiar and easy subject position to occupy (Warin and Dempster, 2007). Warin and Dempster (2007, 901) concluded that:

> The emerging picture is one of laddishness as an easy, comfortable form of social currency in the early days of university where a key goal is to fit in and be accepted among a friendship group and where the biggest anxiety is to end up lonely.

However, although laddism was presented in many ways as easy, 'lad' was not an identity that their interviewees embraced unambiguously. Rather, many presented their laddish performances as inauthentic, as not their 'true selves'. Many spoke about laddism as something they performed strategically to avoid the threat of exclusion by peers. They also suggested that they could reduce the 'inauthentic laddish front' *to some degree* as they settled into university: once they made friends they could be 'more themselves'.

On the one hand, these men's ambivalence to laddism and their attempts to distance themselves from it are heartening. They offer hope and provide potential spaces for resistance and rupture. On the other hand, such narratives are riven with contradictions, tensions, and complexity: these men still perform laddism in some contexts while claiming a different, non-laddish 'authentic' self. There is a disconnect between their self-reported identity and their behaviours (Ford, 2011). Their reluctance in the interviews to fully embrace a 'lad' identity may reflect a number of factors other than a genuine desire to challenge laddism. There is considerable 'jockeying for position' in masculine hierarchies (Edley and Wetherell, 1997), and those who perform hegemonic masculinity in a given context are frequently critiqued, often in private, by those men who do not. This may not always be driven by feminist or pro-feminist goals, but in many cases is done by men in an attempt to self-enhance and jostle for a better position in the masculine hierarchy. For example, in Dempster's (2007) work those who were 'too laddish' – notably the men's rugby and football teams – were Othered as 'superficial', 'thugs', and 'dickheads'. They were cast by Dempster's (middle-class, male) interviewees as inauthentic (see also Gill, 2003). Furthermore, their excessive performances of laddishness were cast, counter-intuitively, as evidence of a dearth of masculinity:

> John: I think … [lads' masculinity] is probably more superficial, perhaps … I think that anything that people think has to be portrayed overtly is possibly in question. It's almost like a reaction to an anxiety about it; it's kind of, they're questioning it themselves, and the easiest way to dispel any interrogation of their masculinity is to

90 *Explanations for Laddism*

overtly show it. And I think I'm more happy in myself perhaps that I don't feel the need to, you know, be part of that.

(Dempster, 2007, 343)

The finding that those who are perceived to be *trying* to be laddish or cool are scorned and identified as 'inauthentic wannabes' is not new. Jackson's (2006a, 99–100) research on laddism in secondary schools, for example, found that 13–14-year-old boys identified the same issues. Jackson's interviewees spoke about the need to be 'effortlessly popular', because those who tried to be popular were ridiculed for it – for trying to be something 'they are not'. Thus, authenticity was again perceived to be crucial, and is reflected also in work in higher education contexts (Diaz-Fernandez and Evans, 2019), including in Dempster's research:

Alex: I don't believe in laddishness ... I believe I can shift my identity to that. But I'm not doing it to show, I'm not doing it to show people, I'm doing it because I enjoy a bit of laddishness you know, just the boys sort of thing.

(Dempster, 2007, 345)

Alex is suggesting here that his laddism is something he dips in and out of, and is one of many identities: 'I can shift my identity to that'. However, he also suggests his laddism, although temporary and contextually contingent, is authentic: he's not laddish 'to show people' – the implication being that others are – rather, when he is laddish it is because 'I enjoy a bit of laddishness'. It is authentic rather than a performance for others. Alex's narrative about shifting identities resonates with Gill's (2003) argument that 'new lad' and 'new man' identities are not fixed identity positions but are discourses or cultural repertoires. Indeed, the ability to switch between 'doing' laddism in some contexts and not in others may be read as an indicator of a skilled cultural actor. As Gill (2003, 39) suggests, the performance of a 'new man' rather than 'new lad' identity may be something men 'knowingly enact to get women into bed'.

According to Dempster (2007), laddism acted as a 'culturally authoritative' discourse through which respondents could verbalise, compare, and evaluate their approaches to masculine self-presentation, and construct a taxonomy of masculine subject positions available in their particular social context. As illustrated earlier, men students' self-narrated relationships to laddism are not straightforward.

Overall, Dempster's research suggested that interviewees were engaged in reconciling the potential benefits of laddishness while attempting to avoid being tarred with the same beer-swilling, loutish, and sexist

Explanations for Laddism 91

brushes as the university's men's rugby and football teams. He argues that laddishness can be seen as a *continuum* of potential gendered subject positionings that exist between two poles: the extreme 'proper' laddishness of rugby and football players, and its less well-defined opposite ('boring', 'lightweight', 'geeky'). Rather than committing to subject positions at either pole and, furthermore, conceptualising these poles as mutually exclusive, fixed, either/or subject positions, the young men in his study moved between the two poles, temporarily practising laddishness *by degree*. This allowed them to dissociate both with the extremities of laddishness and with the undesirable 'lightweight' or 'geek' subject position. Indeed, the majority of interviewees rejected subject positions at either end of the laddish continuum and attempted to find a balanced or 'ordinary' subject position, usually through balancing their academic behaviours with an active social life (cf. Frosh, Phoenix and Pattman, 2002; Jackson, 2006a). This positioning and balancing was also evident in Jeffries' (2019) research: his 'lads' dissociated themselves from the extreme 'anti-academic lads' and were damning of them, depicting them as 'time wasters' (p. 15).

But They're Not Really like That

Authenticity was also a strong discourse among our interviewees. Most staff in our research regarded laddism as not reflecting who a man 'really is'. They tended to cast laddism, and the men, as 'innocent' and sexism and racism as 'not really meant'.

> Even lads participating in this, I do find it very concerning that they send all these pictures. But I genuinely find, I'm thinking of some of the people that you're very familiar with in particular, there's an innocence behind them. When they're separated from the rest of the pack so to speak, they actually have a really genuine, it's almost a schizophrenic idea really, because when they're all together they all collaborate in this huge pretension of, oh they have no respect for women, massive tits, go and bang her, blah blah blah. But when they're separate, or they've got their own partner, their respect comes in, they're aware that you can't behave like that, that it's inappropriate, they know deep down. I think it's just when they get together and feed off each other.
>
> (John, man, focus group, U5)

> The peer pressure and the need to fit in for students as well, it's very easy to get dragged along when they first arrive at university and it's their hall going out to drink and things like that and encouraging people in their flats to drink and things like this. And I think people

92   *Explanations for Laddism*

think well I need to fit in, I need to do this and then regret it because it's not necessarily the way they would behave.

(Marion, woman, U4)

There are notable problems with such accounts. The interviewees present laddish students as innocent and being coerced to behave in ways that are really 'not them' and 'out of character'. Indeed, men's vulnerability was expressed explicitly in some cases: 'I can see where you've got people living away from home for the first time, being thrown into a mix of people who they're not familiar with, wanting to fit in, wanting to make friendship groups, I can see how those people may be vulnerable. And things just become normalised' (Sandra, woman, U1). Such 'poor boys' discourses present men as victims and fail to recognise the patriarchal dividend that men accrue from male power and privilege. We acknowledge the difficulties that many students face when they leave home for the first time and are cast into a new environment where they need to make friends and cope with new demands. Furthermore, we recognise that navigating laddish masculinities and the 'guy code' (Kimmel, 2008) is challenging and often painful for many men. However, portraying men who perform laddism as innocent, vulnerable participants in activities that they really do not want to be involved in, and that do not represent who they 'really are', serves largely to maintain male privilege and the status quo. Furthermore, such 'poor boys' discourses disregard the experiences of women who face many of the same challenges as men in terms of making friends and fitting it, but who have the additional challenge of navigating spaces in which sexual harassment and violence are prevalent.

We also challenge the notion that was dominant in our and Dempster's (2007) interviews, and is dominant in popular discourse more generally, that people have authentic, 'true selves'. As Warin (2010, 35) notes, the notion that 'identity is located within the individual and is waiting to be discovered or liberated from repression' is promoted by many psychologists, counsellors, therapists and self-help gurus. As such, it is a dominant popular discourse; self-help books profess to help us to 'find our true self'. Such notions also emphasise the self as individual, stable over time and across different contexts, and unified in a consistent whole (Warin, 2010). The notion of having one 'true' self that is strong, consistent, and predictable seems to hold considerable appeal in popular discourse, and it is certainly profitable for the 'psy specialists' listed earlier. Indeed, not only is one stable, consistent self valorised in popular and psychological discourses, but the notion of multiple selves is often pathologised (e.g. in misleading yet popular discourses about schizophrenia).

However, as Warin (2010, 36) neatly summarises, post-structuralist academics have problematised and deconstructed the concept of identity. Post-structuralist theorists suggest there is 'no continuous self that can be carried from one social situation to another because the self does not exist outside the social relationships within which it is created'. Thus, post-structuralists argue we have multiple selves, identities, or subjectivities that are socially produced and always in process; they are never complete. So rather than saying these men are 'not like this really', it is better to recognise that we can all adopt different subject positions at different times. Identities are fluid and shifting, contextually contingent. This means that men do not always behave laddishly, but when they do it needs to be analysed rather than simply discounted as 'they don't mean it really', 'it's not really who they are'. Indeed, as referred to earlier in this chapter, Gill (2003, 39) suggests that in some situations it may be the non-laddish performances that are knowingly and cynically enacted to 'get women into bed'. Thus, we need to look beyond explanations that deny or trivialise laddish behaviours, and to focus instead on the structural and cultural contexts and factors that make this behaviour seem acceptable or necessary, and to scrutinise who are the winners and losers. Otherwise, there is a tendency to render invisible the toxic masculine cultures where such behaviours are fostered and encouraged. Unfortunately, as we have noted, many of our interviewees trivialised or minimalised laddism, including by casting it as 'just banter'.

It's Only Banter, They Don't Mean It

A related way in which laddism was presented as not reflecting men's 'true selves' was to dismiss it as light-hearted fun that was not meant seriously. As we began to discuss in Chapter 2, this applied particularly to 'jokes' and banter, as Phil suggests:

> And that kind of thing of: "actually it was just, I don't really mean it, I'm not really racist, I'm not really sexist, I'm just having a laugh, I'm just having a joke. Why are you taking it so seriously?"
>
> (Phil, man, U5)

The racist and sexist 'jokes' that Phil mentions are referred to as 'disparagement humour'. As O'Connor, Ford, and Banos (2017, 568) point out:

> Disparagement humor represents a paradox because it simultaneously communicates two conflicting messages. It communicates both an explicit message of denigration of a target, along with an implicit message that the denigration is free of prejudicial motives or malicious intentions—it's 'just a joke' meant to amuse and not to be taken seriously ... Humor thus provides a cover story of social acceptability for expressions of prejudice and malice that allows it to avert the standard challenges or opposition that non-humorous disparagement likely would incur ... Although expressed under the

94   *Explanations for Laddism*

cover of social acceptability, disparagement humor represents a subtle expression of prejudice; it communicates shared stereotypes and antagonistic attitudes toward a social group.

Research in a variety of contexts has demonstrated the ways in which humour, and especially disparagement humour, is employed in the construction of masculine hierarchies – both intra- and intergroup – and is inextricably linked to power. Jeffries (2019, 8) notes how the self-identified lads in his research gained kudos from being quick witted, and especially at a friend's expense. Some of our interviewees identified this, and explained laddism as men: 'wanting to seem like the top dog, the alpha male, "I'm the one with the best jokes, I'm the one with the most girls after me"' (Sally, woman, U5). Walker and Goodson (1977, 214) suggest that '[s]uccess or failure at telling jokes endangers status in the immediate context and so not surprisingly it is usually those with most power in the situation who tell most jokes' (see also Kehily and Nayak, 1997). Our interviewees commented on the ways in which high status men would instigate chants and jokes within their group, thus indicating and reinforcing the group hierarchy, as well as instantiating the group culture and norms: 'We seem to find it's one leader of the club that will start the chants or make the jokes and because we have a lot of first years that are quite new to it, and feel they need to fit in, they will follow very much' (Sophie, woman, U3). Homophobic 'jokes', for example, reinforce heteronormativity: they demean non-heterosexual men and concomitantly consolidate the heterosexual masculinity of the teller and the rest of the group (Kehily and Nayak, 1997; Rawlings, 2019). Chants work in similar ways.

In Chapter 3 we explored in depth the narrative of one of our interviewees who encountered her university's men's rugby union club chanting misogynistic and racist lines on a public bus. This was not the only instance raised in our research, another example related to chants by members of an elite university about students at a neighbouring post-1992 university: 'Elitism. One of the chants that they have been heard singing on [name of] Road was "[chanting letters of name of another university in the city], one day you will work for me" about [name of other university] students' (Chloe, woman, U6). Cheeseman (2010, 150) discusses similar chants based on his ethnographic research at Sheffield University. Noting that there were 15 derogatory chants by Sheffield University students (a Russell Group University) about Sheffield Hallam students (a post-1992 university), and only one about Sheffield University students chanted by Sheffield Hallam students, he argues that the status stratification:

> explains the preponderance of anti-Hallam chants as all are adaptations of those used at football matches (Luhrs, 2007). Because

fans typically taunt each other over their lack of intelligence, wealth and morality, sexual or otherwise (Widdowson, 1981; Luhrs, 2007), there are more chants on these subjects for Sheffield students to adapt. Due to the perceived stratification of the HE system, Hallam students are thus left with a poverty of response. This perfectly demonstrates the highly competitive, instrumental and banter-sodden atmosphere of HE, where students are desperate for identity and find it in the aggressive liquidity markets at the expense of any sense of solidarity....

When challenged about the chanting, Cheeseman reports that students brushed it off as just a joke. Research by social psychologists shows how chants such as these and disparagement humour more generally serve to denigrate 'out-groups' and thereby simultaneously enhance the status of the 'in-group', as well as distancing the ingroup from the outgroup. For example, jokes told by men that denigrate women serve both to position women as different from, and inferior to, men (O'Connor, Ford and Banos, 2017). This is very explicit in the elitist chants of Sheffield University students about their counterparts at Sheffield Hallam. In this chant the (ex)polytechnic history of Sheffield Hallam is used to suggest that it is not a university at all:

> I go somewhere you don't go!
> Uni! Uni!
> I go somewhere you don't go!
> Uni-ver-si-ty!

Thus, disparagement humour is used to boost the power and status of certain groups, and also certain members within them, at the expense of others. Furthermore, as Cheeseman (2010) notes, more powerful groups tend to have more ammunition at their disposal. Yet couching derogatory comments as humour makes them more difficult to challenge, as the boundaries between humour and harassment are blurred by that process (Kehily and Nayak, 1997). Those who challenge such jokes are Othered and subject to (further) attack as humourless killjoys, a refrain frequently targeted at feminists (Phipps and Young, 2015a). Some of our interviewees commented on the ways in which weaving in jokiness protected privileged men from accusations of racism, sexism, homophobia, and so on:

> I think that's where this jokey element to it comes from, that they're educated and privileged enough to be aware that some of this stuff may be distasteful to others. Which is why they've weaved in this jokey element, because it protects them from being accused of the isms we've just talked about ... I think it's just so normalised that actually most people - and many women as well, I'm not saying it's

96   *Explanations for Laddism*

just men - will say, 'oh it's just guys having a laugh, that's what guys do'. And that I think is the biggest challenge really, how do you address that normalisation?

(Jessica, woman, U2)

The challenge that Jessica highlights is an important one; the normalisation of sexist, racist, and homophobic humour contributes to a toxic culture in which there is a continuum of harassment and violence. Thomae and Pina (2015, 197), for example, highlight how Ryan and Kanjorski's (1998) work demonstrates 'clear links between men's enjoyment of sexist humor and their rape myth acceptance, self-reported likelihood of forcing sex and psychological, physical and sexual relationship aggression'.

Furthermore, Jeffries' (2019) interviews with seven students who self-identified as lads support Jessica's argument that laddish students are 'educated and privileged enough to be aware that some of this stuff may be distasteful to others'. The narratives of Jeffries' interviewees conveyed a complex and nuanced understanding of the uses and effects of banter. Jeffries (2019, 11) concludes that 'Banter was a key aspect of the interviewees' friendships. They were absolutely clear that banter only works between friends and that banter aimed at other people was insulting and bullying'. Thus, it seems much more likely that banter is part of a calculated and cynical performance of laddism rather than being performed by naïve, unknowing young men as Josh (man, U3) portrayed in Chapter 2: 'And they would be mortified if they ever thought for a second that somebody thought they were intentionally going out to be homophobic or sexist'.

Other Trivialising and Essentialising Discourses

I think a lot of it is passed off as boys will be boys kind of thing.

(Will, man, U5)

So far in this chapter we have explored the discourse that laddism is an easy and accessible identity for men university students, particularly during the transition to university. Relatedly, we explored the idea that performing laddism does not reflect who men 'really are', but rather is (a) an inauthentic front adopted to 'fit in' and/or (b) light-hearted fun that is not meant seriously; it's largely jokey and humorous. We problematised both of these notions by challenging the idea of a single, authentic identity and exploring the ways in which disparagement humour serves to build and reinforce masculine status hierarchies at the expense of those who are Othered. Interviewees also drew on other discourses to explain laddism that individualised and trivialised it: these were often age (and gender) related.

Explanations for Laddism 97

> It could be age, I don't know, yeah it could be an age thing. Because, I mean remember that the early 20s, it's when we're all trying to form relationships with each other and you know, whether that's friendship or romantic relationships and interpreting behaviour over the line and not over the line is a very difficult business when you're in that position I think. So I think it's probably more prominent in younger students because they're more insecure about gender relationships.
>
> (Heather, woman, U6)

> It's always something that surprises me, is that immaturity emotionally and about thinking about other people and the impact your behaviour has on other people ... and then coming out and having the freedom to explore different cultures and different ways of life and everything. They sometimes have that kind of, it seems to manifest itself in a sort of, a version of laddism when they get here sometimes.
>
> (Marion, woman, U4)

These types of explanation again work to essentialise laddism. Rather than exploring the cultures that create and sustain laddish masculinities, they present it as something inherent in individual men that is age as well as gender related. Some interviewees, although they were a minority, commented on how such essentialist explanations served to discursively reduce men's responsibility: 'sometimes it's used as an excuse: "oh they're just boys". I've got three nephews and I think they get away with a lot because "oh it's just boys, that's how boys behave"' (Rebecca, woman, U4). Explanations that serve to essentialise men's behaviours have been severely critiqued over many years by feminists. For example, for decades feminists have debunked essentialist arguments that men's rape of women may be explained in relation to men's 'uncontrollable sexual urges' and have focused instead on gendered power relations (Brownmiller, 1975). However, essentialist explanations remain relatively strong in popular discourse and were strong in our research in relation to all aspects of lad culture. A notable example related to a student who was described as 'behaving completely inappropriately with women'. There were a series of allegations about the student, some of which were dealt with by the police, including grabbing a woman round the throat and serious sexual assault. In conversation with the university his family were said to explain his behaviours in terms of him being freed from the restrictions and constraints of his previous environment: 'They put it down to ... the environment he was in in Turkey [was] very restricted, very controlled, and coming to a very liberal western city gave him the opportunity to' (Pete, man, U2). The essentialism conveyed in this dialogue is stark – it conveys a portrait of a man whose inner being will drive him to abuse women if 'given the opportunity'. Again, similar

98 Explanations for Laddism

to discourses about the freedom afforded by university in general, there is a pernicious essentialism embedded here (see also Phipps, 2017a).

There are interesting contradictions in the explanations we have explored so far. On the one hand, there are strong discourses about laddish men 'not really being like that', that not being who they 'really are', which are also related to explanations about them 'only joking'. On the other hand, however, there are also dominant essentialist discourses about 'boys will be boys' and that's what men do. While contradictory, they nevertheless have similar effects – they position men as not responsible, either because they 'can't help it', or because it's not a true reflection of who they 'really are'. Such discourses were also bolstered by the associations between lad culture and alcohol:

> People may not realise it's not okay if they're drunk, people may not realise they're doing it … I think it's down to the sexual desires and the need for people to find a partner. And just it comes out, when there's this laddish behaviour it comes out in the wrong way, because their judgement is impaired by alcohol and they forget that the normal things can happen. You don't have to grab someone if you want them kind of thing.
>
> (Naomi, woman, U3)

As discussed in previous chapters, laddism was strongly associated with alcohol, and alcohol was seen as a vehicle for laddish behaviours (see also Dempster, 2011). Furthermore, laddish behaviours were often attributed to alcohol: it was argued that men would not behave so laddishly without it. This sentiment was expressed by Naomi earlier, as well as by numerous other interviewees who placed a strong emphasis on alcohol, and in some cases drugs, for removing inhibitions.

> I think drinking's a given. I don't think you would see the same amounts of lad culture if people didn't lose their inhibitions through that … I think drinking has a part to play in it. I think it probably has a huge part to play in it and I think there is a big issue in what drinking leads to in terms of lack of inhibitions.
>
> (Phil, man, U5)

While we acknowledge that alcohol has a variety of pharmacological effects, like Pedersen, Copes, and Sandberg (2016, 557) we argue that we also need to consider the 'situational factors and cultural norms regarding how to behave while intoxicated'. Focusing on the link between alcohol and violence, Pedersen et al. (2016) highlight a body of research which suggests that 'drunken behaviour (including violence) is determined in large part by cultural rules rather than just pharmacological changes'. Thus, they argue that we need to consider how cultural

Explanations for Laddism 99

values and beliefs concerning violence and aggression intersect with those about alcohol. This includes interrogating the social and cultural ways in which gender, masculinity, and power are constructed and performed in such settings. Calls to interrogate these aspects are echoed by Graham, Wilson, and Taft (2017), who argue that highly masculinised drinking environments may provide potential perpetrators of, in their case alcohol-related intimate partner violence (AIPV), with 'the environmental permission and temporal cues that make AIPV more likely' (p. 11). Although Pedersen et al.'s (2016) research is conducted in a different national context (Norway) from ours, and they focus on violence in general rather than specifically on gender-based violence and harassment, their findings and conclusions are pertinent to our research and national context (both countries are considered to be within the 'binge drinking belt' of Europe). Through their lengthy, in-depth interviews with 104 young adult 'binge drinkers', they highlight the ways in which violence was expected in nightclubs and at parties where people are drinking. Furthermore,

> The violence is partly due to alcohol itself and partly due to the effect the substance is perceived to have by those in the drinking culture where normative transgressions are valued ... alcohol sparks violence, but it is transmitted through a drinking culture that expects transgressions when drunk.
>
> (p. 560)

The implications of this are important, as they argue that preventative work would usefully focus on changing expectations about violence in these contexts, and on mobilising forms of masculinity and femininity that reduce violence. Furthermore, by understanding the ways in which some forms of violence are expected in these contexts and explained and excused by drink, we can begin to work to challenge these expectations and excuses. In our research such expectations and explanations were common.

> Some of those things that you've been taught socially that inhibit you from saying things that might cause offence, and so the kind of drugs or the drink remove all of those social inhibitions that have been put there for good reason. You strip those away and then it's like Lord of Flies isn't it? It's just you've got a bunch of people on an island who don't care what they do to each other and so it gets messy and nasty.
>
> (Olivia, woman, U3)

They all drink before they go out now because drinks are so expensive in clubs. So they're sort of a bit tanked up before they even go

100   *Explanations for Laddism*

out. And maybe that leads to, I'm sure that leads to abuses, because you have got people that are inevitably more vulnerable.

(Martha, woman, U2)

We pick up the implications of such discourses more fully in Chapter 5.

Lad Culture in Teaching/Learning Spaces

The strong associations between alcohol, the night-time economy, and laddism meant that many of our interviewees failed to see or even consider the ways in which laddism permeated teaching/learning contexts, as conveyed by Will (man, U5): 'So I think when [there is] alcohol and the club environment or the public environment, you can do things that you wouldn't do obviously in the academic setting'. However, as noted in Chapter 2, although lad culture was more likely overall to be associated with social spaces, this varied between institutions according to student demographics and the physical estate of the universities. We noted that lad culture tended to be identified as an issue in *social spaces* more often when institutions recruited predominantly 'traditional' students who lived on or close to the university and where there was a vibrant social scene locally. It was presented as less of an issue in social spaces in institutions where students were predominantly 'non-traditional'. The 'non-traditional' make-up of the student population was associated with lower levels of laddish behaviour as these students were perceived by staff not to engage in typical student nightlife and drinking cultures due to their age, family responsibilities, living away from the university, religious beliefs, or cultural differences. In some cases the university (especially U2 and also U1) was presented as not set up to provide the 'traditional experience' for 18-year-olds:

> Some of our courses, arts in particular, would attract students nationally. Other courses are very, very local. So we're a local university for some courses and some of the students live at home and they just come in to study ... I mean if you picked other universities, I mean. I've got children who are going off to university, so the last year or so I've been going round with my wife and then you see different universities. ... We went to [name of pre-1992 university] a couple of times and the vast majority of people from [name of university] were, I would say, from the 18-to-19-year-old bracket, and were leaving home for the first time and going to university, and that was part of that rite of passage. We certainly don't have that here for the vast majority of our students. It's not that experience that we offer and are geared up to offer.

(Pete, man, U2)

Explanations for Laddism 101

As noted in Chapter 2, in institutions where there were predominantly 'non-traditional' students, lad culture was more often seen to be an issue in teaching/learning contexts (especially in U2), whereas this was far less commonly referred to in the institutions with a predominantly 'traditional' student demographic (universities 4–6). However, there were a few instances of classroom lad culture in pre-1992 institutions, and our data seem to reflect Phipps' (2017a) observation that there are differences in the forms of classroom laddism between elite and non-elite universities (see Chapter 2). A common theme throughout participants' discourses around laddism in teaching/learning spaces was that it was levelled primarily at women lecturers, thus underscoring the gendered basis for such harassment and abuse. Furthermore, and as we have seen elsewhere, sexism was in some cases coupled with racism or homophobia, as the second exchange below illustrates.

> I can certainly think back over the years where I've felt a bit challenged by groups of boys in the class, and it usually is male students rather than female students ... Yeah, I can just think of loads of male students that were quite challenging at times. I used to have one that used to come in and sit down and read the newspaper. And I actually sent him to see, I think I sent him to the programme director because I couldn't think of who to send him to in this context. And he used to deliberately do it to kind of wind me up kind of stuff and I can't imagine a female student doing that, I haven't ever experienced that.
>
> (Heather, woman, U6)

> Paul: A good friend of mine who was a colleague of my girlfriend taught at [name of University] and on the feedback - she taught EU law - and on the feedback somebody had written 'I shouldn't have to learn EU law, I shouldn't have to learn EU law from this blond-haired, blue-eyed fucking Nazi.' Because she was German. Regularly, I mean I've heard people, members of staff, referred to as immigrants.
>
> Interviewer: Really?
>
> Paul: On feedback forms, yes. Talking about a Greek member of staff saying ... if we're going to be taught by an immigrant then they should be able to speak English without an accent.
>
> (Paul, man, focus group, U5)

Feedback forms afford students anonymity, and there is mounting evidence that women lecturers are judged differently and more harshly than their men counterparts (MacNell, Driscoll and Hunt, 2015; Mitchell and Martin, 2018). While student feedback was not a focus in our interviews, a few interviewees cited anonymous module evaluations as a vehicle for some students to express racist and misogynist views. Another

102   *Explanations for Laddism*

example which was noted in Chapter 2 was a woman lecturer who had been described as 'MILF' [Mother I'd like to fuck] on an anonymous feedback form (Pete, man, U2).

The types of classroom laddism that involved more visible disruptive behaviour or refusal to engage with academic work in lectures were reported as more common in the post-1992 institutions, especially in U2. Such behaviours, which parallel the ways laddism has been described in school contexts, included coming to class without having prepared to participate or contribute to academic discussion, frequent interruptions to the lecture/lecturer, heckling or undermining the lecturer or other students in the session:

> general disruption, poor behaviour in class which is everything from turning up late or leaving early or wandering in and out in a disruptive way, to lack of preparation so arriving not only without having done the reading or the preparation but without a pen, that sort of thing ... but the disruptive classroom behaviour does seem to be overwhelmingly, though not exclusively, a male student problem.
>
> (Elsa, woman, U2)

As well as being more frequently reported in post-1992 universities, it was also reported to be more common in some disciplines than others, most notably in management schools and sports-related areas, both of which are highly 'masculine' domains (see also Jackson et al., 2015; Stentiford, 2019). As part of her role, Sue (U2) undertook observations of teaching across the university, and she highlighted the areas where laddism was most rife.

> The most extreme forms of behaviour I see tend to be in the business school 'cos that's often where the large cohorts are. So let's check some specific examples, strategic management, law - there's been many challenges with our groups of law students - human resource management. Sport - there has been an ongoing thing ... there's a couple of female lecturers who would be able to articulate very convincingly the challenges that they see and they manage it very differently from their male counterparts. And there's a couple who manage it really really well, you know very effective teachers and there are male lecturers who collude with the male students and allow, you know, women students are a tiny minority, to be harassed and bullied.
>
> (Sue, Woman, U2)

In their discussion of disruptive laddish practices in sports science (Jackson, Dempster and Pollard, 2015) and in higher education more generally (Burke et al., 2013), Jackson et al. and Burke et al. rightly stress

Explanations for Laddism   103

the importance of considering the intersections of gender, ethnicity, age, and social class for understanding such disruptive practices, which are undertaken predominantly by young men. While our data do not enable us to explore discipline differences in detail, it is important to attempt to understand how the causes of laddism may differ depending on who is performing it (Phipps, 2017a), the context in which it occurs, and the forms it takes. For example, Burke et al. (2013, 40) argue that disruptive behaviour by some students may be seen as a form of alienation, arguing that:

> Utilising this concept [alienation] can help to explain the behaviour of some students in terms of coming to lectures late; talking at the back of the lecture theatre; texting throughout, all of which lecturers and students highlighted as problematic. This behaviour could be construed as refusing to adopt the "good student" subjectivity (Grant 1997) but what it actually points to is the need for lecturers to look afresh at teaching styles and the context of learning in which some students are being marginalised.

This chimes with some of Sue's observations who, although very critical of laddism, acknowledges the ways in which students' sexism and racism can collide with poor curriculum planning to create the perfect storm, in this case for a young, Chinese woman lecturer.

> 'What needs to be understood is, I think we create situations through how we deliver the curriculum where those behaviours are most likely to flourish. So they had a 24-week Masters module, an aspect of management, two-hour lecture each week, no seminars and I think they were about 110 in number. Young Chinese lecturer, very able researcher, you know she'd planned a good session, but two hours is too long, you know you're limited in terms of interactivity, these are things you really need to have a seminar environment to explore fully. We were 20 weeks in to a 24-week course, I counted and I counted and I counted. We started off at 4pm with 12 students out of 100. Over the course of the next hour they started to come in and they kept coming, so every five minutes there's a new interruption. No apology, no embarrassment, no regard for the people who are there for the lecturer ... And they proceeded to talk and to heckle when questions were asked. It wasn't a great session but it wasn't the worst. So I was quite taken aback by the scale of it ... I've never seen in the last year a session where so many students have been so disengaged and so rude and so disrespectful and that thing about not valuing the teacher ... because they were like 'I can't hear, I can't hear' and these were people who had been talking. And the implication [was she was inaudible] because she was Chinese.

104 *Explanations for Laddism*

And you know, I could hear her, I was right at the back. But they were saying that to undermine and to unsettle [her] and of course what happened was ... she loses confidence and you can see it drain away. So our conversation afterwards, it was just a formative teaching observation, we talked about a curriculum which sets up a situation which ... it's just impossible to manage unless you're incredibly charismatic, unless you can really hold the crowd, have really determined those rules of engagement early and are able to maintain that. And we talked about some strategies that she could use. But unless you have a departmental approach to managing this, and some kind of contracting, but we're in that really weird situation where postgraduate students give us a lot of income, but how can you manage people in a great big group? You can't. So actually you shouldn't be offering two-hour lectures, you should be running seminars ... She was finding the whole experience disempowering. She was questioning her own ability and no-one was there to support and help her and then what you start doing is start blaming the students and actually, yeah, there is some accountability there, they shouldn't be behaving in that way. But they're bored, they're disappointed and in a sense there's a level of collusion because by not challenging it, you're saying it's okay.

(Sue, woman, U2)

In the same institution, one programme had shifted all their teaching from lectures to seminars because they had experienced disruption in lectures. The interviewee narrating this shift was of the opinion that other programmes experienced more disruption, but these programme staff were particularly responsive to student dis/engagement.

We've certainly had one subject area which has given up large group lectures because the degree, try as they might, they could not train, if you like, students to engage with the lecture in the traditional way that they felt the lecture needed to be engaged with, to work as a lecture. So they've simply stopped doing large group lectures, moved that time into smaller group seminars, group project sessions and re-cast the learning around that. ... Part of the reason that they decided to abandon the lectures is that they are very responsive to what students seem to be telling them. So they haven't so much said 'well if you don't want to listen we're walking away', it's much more a kind of the fact that the students are not engaging and seem not to value this time, [which] indicates that this is not the right way to teach them, so we'll stop doing it. It's taken the disruption as a signal of disengagement or something. Whereas perhaps other subject areas, either because they haven't got the flexibility to drop the lectures or because they feel much more strongly that the lectures are a really

Explanations for Laddism   105

important teaching method, persist with it in spite of what might be quite serious disruptive behaviour

(Elsa, woman, U2)

Elsa noted too that disruption seemed to have increased in the last five to six years, and there had been discussions within the institution about why this might have been the case. Staff seemed to think a number of factors contributed to it, including students having higher expectations because they were now paying high fees and 'a refusal to be bored' (Elsa, woman, U2).

It is difficult to disentangle the various factors that may be at work, as they intersect in complex ways. There is an important body of work highlighting the ways in which working-class students, in particular, feel out of place at university, and do not know how to 'play the game' or are unwilling to do so (Bathmaker et al., 2016; Abrahams, 2017; Reay, 2017). These sentiments are evident in Elsa's (U2) narrative: 'they could not train, if you like, students to engage with the lecture in the traditional way'. Research suggests that some working-class men especially can be resistant to higher education cultures. For example, based on several projects that involved working with non-higher education participants – either teenagers who were still at school or young adults who had chosen not to go into higher education – Louise Archer (2006) argued that boys and men in her samples constructed going to university as undesirable and incompatible with working-class masculinities. This resulted from a combination of factors, notably, higher education was constructed as feminised; associated with undesirable forms of middle-class masculinity; and seen as oppositional to performances of popular, 'cool' masculinities. Thus, it is possible that some men's disruptive behaviours in class at U2 and elsewhere are a reaction to a university context in which they feel alienated, one they perceive as feminised, middle class, and 'uncool'. Thus, perhaps universities should be working harder to accommodate the needs of this group of students whose disruptive behaviour may be a sign of alienation and resistance to a system in which they are Othered. On the other hand, as Jackson, Dempster, and Pollard (2015) argue, it's important that we do not respond only to the needs of vocal, disruptive men at the expense of women or, indeed, less vocal men.

What is clear, however, is that we need to recognise different forms of lad culture and theorise them differently depending on the context and perpetrators (Phipps, 2017a). Furthermore, lad culture in higher education should be considered beyond its forms and impacts in social spaces. Its occurrence in teaching/learning spaces appears not only to have consequences for women students, but impacts on staff experiences too. Understanding the varied and in some cases subtle ways in which lad culture permeates higher education contexts allows us to think about the settings in which sexism operates in more insidious, less overt ways.

106 *Explanations for Laddism*

Gender, Power, and Competition

> I interpret it as humorous in quotation marks, gendered aggression.
>
> (Lisa, woman, U4)

While discourses that trivialise laddism were dominant among our interviewees, they were not the only ones. Some interviewees – most notably those whose professional or personal interests related to gender, equality, and diversity – offered gendered and sometimes intersectional analyses. These analyses focused primarily upon the maintenance of (white, middle-class, heterosexual) male privilege and on competitive cultures of masculinities.

> Interviewer: Have you any thoughts about what you think motivates laddism?
>
> That's a difficult one. I think there's probably like an unconscious motivation and that's just kind of maintaining the status quo of male privilege. I don't know whether men who actually act in this way would actually think about it like that, but I think the root cause of it is just generally kind of male supremacy in society and this dominant masculinity and a general misogyny and disrespect towards women and all of those kind of factors. But I don't know on a more personal, tangible level why men choose to do that. I guess it's the way that a lot of men are just taught to socialise and interact maybe and it's about power probably.
>
> (Chloe, woman, U6)

> Interviewer: What do you think motivates it [lad culture]?
>
> I think there are a couple of elements to it. One, wildly speculating, I think it's the continuation of male privilege: 'I'm entitled and able to do this and I want to carry on doing this and it feels good'. You know, actually booze and drugs and sport and sex for many people are highly pleasurable, exciting things. And to be part of a shared experience with other men - and maybe even some women but mainly men - who reinforce that and you feel good about yourself, I can see that's highly attractive to some people … I just think it's motivated by - because they can! Because actually there's very little that challenges it and it is still seen as aspirational for many men to have a fast car, lots of money, to do masculine activities like sport and adventuring things and to have a beautiful plastic woman on your arm who does whatever you want her to do. And that's really strongly reinforced throughout society.
>
> (Jessica, woman, U2)

These interviewees begin to analyse laddism in relation to prevailing societal power structures (continuation of male privilege) as well as its

Explanations for Laddism   107

appeals at the individual level (pleasure and excitement). Analyses that work across different levels – individual to societal/global – are especially valuable (Jackson, 2010b). Chloe (U6) and Jessica (U2) both highlight the maintenance of patriarchy as a powerful motivator for laddism. Lisa (U4) voiced a similar view:

> Well, a general belief that women are inferior to men lies at the base of it despite the fact that we've changed a lot of things as a society around it. That's the underlying cause of it and that hasn't changed as much as I think people think.

While the maintenance of patriarchy was an explanation offered by a minority of participants, a desire for power more generally was voiced by more of our interviewees: 'I guess thinking that you're powerful and thinking that you can dominate what other people do. I'm sure those are big motivators and I think yeah, it is kind of power over other people' (Diana, woman, U4). Such explanations were inextricably linked to competition and a desire for status: 'I think wanting to seem like the top dog, the alpha male, I'm the one with the best jokes, I'm the one with the most girls after me' (Sally, woman, U5). This explanation ties closely to issues discussed earlier in the chapter about dominant masculinities, the need to fit in, and transition to university. Jason's comments encapsulate all of these elements:

> Because they are, especially the first years, they're here, they've got to make friends, they need to present an image of themselves and that [image] with the boys will quite often be who's the most macho, who's the hardest, who's slept with the most girls, who can tell the most offensive joke.
>
> (Jason, man, U5)

Jason elucidates laddism as being underpinned by competition and a need to be the 'most masculine'. Jackson (2006a) has argued that competition and fear of social and academic failure are key to understanding laddism in secondary schools, and we suggest that they play an important role in higher education contexts too. Ella (woman, U2), for example, narrated competition and fear as key motivators for laddism at university: 'For me I would say the main motivation is competition and fear is also part of it; it's like competition and fear are the same things, let's face it. For me it is about competition'. Phipps and Young (2015a) have made a similar argument, linking competition particularly to the neoliberalisation of higher education. Defining neoliberalism as 'a value system in which the economic has replaced the intellectual and political and in which the competitive, rational individual predominates over the collective', Phipps and Young (2015a) argue that neoliberalism is intensifying and creating

108 *Explanations for Laddism*

new modes of competition. Furthermore, they argue that the neoliberal higher education context has made laddism more brutal as 'neoliberalism is a culture of "cruelty and harsh competitiveness"' (pp. 315–316). Thus, they argue that neoliberalism, which places all responsibility on individuals for their successes and failures, intensifies pressures to succeed, to be the best, to have the most (see also Nyström, Jackson and Salminen Karlsson, 2019). Our analyses support this argument, which was also reflected in the comments of some of our interviewees:

> Pressure I think, pressure to be, yes to be the heart and soul of the party, to be the cleverest, the fittest and yeah, a culture where you have to show that to others, and I think that's partly demonstrated by the success of social media. You have to be seen to be successful, you can't be successful on the quiet, and success is measured in terms of physical beauty and the amount of partners you have.
>
> (Ella, woman, U2)

> Does it get more extreme? Yes it gets more extreme in that they egg each other on. But it gets, I say it gets more extreme, it gets more ridiculous, it gets to the point where they're snogging a pig's head in a pub in town somewhere ... but even going back six, seven years we would get those physical competitions. You'd get the rugby league and the rugby union having a scrap because nobody wanted to stand down, you know, and it was that macho thing which feeds into lad culture, I guess.
>
> (Josh, man, U3)

Summary

We were heartened by the ways in which some of our interviews, albeit a very small minority, offered an analysis of lad culture that acknowledged the structural gender inequalities that underpin it. This was in stark contrast to the majority who explained lad culture in gender-blind ways that served to render invisible the gender norms, expectations, and structural intersecting inequalities that we argue underpin and sustain lad culture. This is not to critique those individual interviewees; their narratives largely reflect representations of lad culture that are dominant in the press and wider society. However, while understandable, such explanations are highly problematic in our opinion. In the next chapter we delineate our argument about why such gender-blind explanations are a problem, and offer an alternative theorisation of lad culture that is founded upon a gendered analysis.

5 (Re)theorising and Addressing Lad Culture

Introduction

In this chapter we contribute to a (re)theorisation of lad culture by drawing on our analysis of staff understandings of what lad culture is, where it occurs, who participates in laddish behaviour, and what are seen to be the underlying causes. We argue that in order for lad culture to be understood and challenged, a (re)theorisation of its underpinnings and the factors that sustain and perpetuate it are essential. We build on recent work in the field by Alison Phipps (2017a) to argue for a theorisation of lad culture that takes into account the hegemony of binary gender relations, the multiple and intersecting ways in which gender is performed, and the role of gendered organisational regimes of higher education institutions in fostering particular values. As we have argued throughout the book, while lad culture is a UK-specific term, the behaviours and attitudes associated with lad culture are most definitely not UK-specific. Thus, our (re)theorising has salience and value well beyond the United Kingdom.

Our data, as well as existing student data, suggest that gender performativity and the maintenance of binary gender relations, including the sexual and social subjugation of women, are key to the perpetuation of lad culture. However, we argue that such features and mechanisms are frequently obfuscated by largely gender-blind analyses, which were dominant among our interviewees, as they are more broadly in popular discourses about laddism. Indeed, as we discussed in Chapters 2 and 3, the ways and spaces in which lad culture was seen – or not – and views about who was seen as laddish, were shaped by particular (often gender-blind) conceptualisations of lad culture. In this chapter, we develop our argument that dominant conceptualisations of lad culture – in the media, among our sample, and in society generally – are underpinned by a largely gender-blind, limited theorisation of how lad culture arises and how it manifests. So, in what follows, we synthesise findings and analyses from previous chapters to highlight what is rendered invisible in the conceptualisations of lad culture that were dominant in our research, and then we offer a way to reconceptualise lad culture that makes visible the gendered norms and expectations that underpin it. In the final part of the chapter we draw on our (re)theorisation of lad culture to critically

110 *(Re)theorising and Addressing Lad Culture*

explore what is being done, and what should be done, to address lad culture in universities.

Conceptualisations of Lad Culture among Our Participants

> I don't think there's a massive laddy, laddy culture. I think it's just, yeah, there's a bit of a laugh and a joke now and again, but that's about it really.
>
> (Ian, man, U2)

An analysis of the gender norms and expectations that underpin and sustain lad culture was largely absent in the narratives of the majority of our participants. This absence has important implications for whether and where lad culture is visible and perceptions about how it should be addressed, or indeed, what is perceived as worthy of being addressed: 'More should *not* be done to tackle lad culture in higher education because it's not a big issue; we've got bigger fish to fry' (Nigel, man, U1). Within this gender-blind framework, lad culture was seen in two main ways.

We noted in Chapters 1 and 2 that lad culture might be seen as a continuum, with 'mild' laddism – for example sexist stereotyping – at one end and extreme forms – such as sexual violence – at the other end. However, in our research, as in previous work (Dempster, 2007), there tended to be an important line of demarcation on this continuum, notably, where the laddism switched to being 'extreme'. So there was in fact something of a dichotomy in terms of how lad culture was conceptualised, which is also reflected in the UK press (Jackson and Sundaram, 2018). One conceptualisation was very broad, where laddism covered a wide spectrum of practices, some more problematic, or problematised, than others. This very broad conceptualisation is typified in Sue's comment:

> I don't know whether that helps in defining lad culture 'cos you could actually say it's almost everything, and it's not just confined to people who are in sports clubs. To me it's behaviour which jars, which grates, which is not respectful.
>
> (Sue, woman, U2)

Conversely, the second conceptualisation portrayed laddism as characterised by very specific, often highly visible 'extreme' practices that became noticeable through their exceptional (exceptionally problematic) status: 'Well, we've had sex attacks. We've had female students being attacked on the way home from the university, all well publicised as well' (Jack, man, U6).[1] We are not suggesting that staff conceptualised it in one way or the other; both were dominant discourses among the narratives of the vast majority interviewees. Furthermore, both discourses fail

(Re)theorising and Addressing Lad Culture 111

to acknowledge the structural and systemic gender inequality that underpins lad culture, instead offering more individualised explanations.

'It's Almost Everything': Lad Culture as Very Broad

When conceptualised broadly, a range of factors were seen to be associated with and to explain laddish behaviour. For example, lad culture was associated with, *inter alia*, sexism, misogyny, racism, homophobia, having a laugh, banter, social spaces such as bars, sport, heavy drinking, objectifying women, being loud and disruptive, sexual harassment, and gender-based violence. Ways in which it was most commonly explained included the need to fit in and peer pressure, being drunk, immaturity, being in a sports team, boys being boys, it's only a joke, among others. We explored these in Chapter 4. Often, the factors associated with lad culture were seen as contexts or vehicles for lad culture as well as explanations for laddish practices. So, spaces in which alcohol consumption was high were seen as key contexts for rowdy, harassing, or even violent behaviour (see also Diaz-Fernandez and Evans, 2019a). Simultaneously, these behaviours were seen as fundamentally linked to alcohol consumption, in the sense that they were narrated as not occurring without it. A similar narrative was deployed in relation to sports teams and rituals: sports team socials were seen as contexts for chanting, banter, and harassment or humiliation. These practices were not easily imagined as taking place outside of this physical/spatial context, or the context of the sports group. So the sports social context itself was narrated as an explanation for these behaviours – the context and group were seen to *produce* laddism.

This was also reflected in Phipps and Young's research (NUS, 2013) who noted that lad culture was identified as a 'pack mentality' by participants in their study; the pack, the setting, the event is the context *and* the explanation for these practices. The identification of specific individual factors as vehicles, and reasons, for lad culture lends itself to a more atomised, and perhaps reactive approach to some of the practices associated with lad culture. If alcohol is imagined to be the underlying problem, for example, then a focus on responsible drinking or management of alcohol consumption may be presented as a solution. Similarly, laddish behaviour by sports teams has often been punished by curtailing engagement in the sport itself, for example, by exclusion from playing in the team for a number of matches. Other responses have been to develop codes of conduct for sports teams. Thus, the locus of the preventative and punitive responses has been the sporting context itself.

An individualised (or group) approach to understanding why particular men (and women) engage in laddish behaviour was taken by most of our participants, rather than seeing these practices as rooted in and as mirroring wider societal and cultural expectations for gender behaviour.

112   (Re)theorising and Addressing Lad Culture

The individualised stance was also evident in narratives about alcohol consumption, sports initiations, and rowdy behaviour: these practices were not analysed in relation to gender norms or expectations for the most part, but were explained in localised terms. The role of gender in the enactment of the range of practices that were described as laddish by university staff was therefore also invisibilised to some extent.

So, despite the gendered nature of the term lad culture, discussions rarely centred on gender as a set of social and cultural expectations. With some notable exceptions, when gender was discussed it tended to be portrayed either in essentialist terms and/or defensively. For example, as we saw in Chapter 4, the 'boys will be boys' discourse was prominent, and lad culture was presented as almost inevitable: 'It can be sexist, but I think if you put lots of men together it's one of the things they will be, they can bond about' (Lucy, woman, U2). We also witnessed a considerable amount of defensiveness on behalf of men, from both men and women:

> The kinds of behaviours are quite varied really. The terminology - lad culture - in itself is quite a sex-biased term, because it's not just lads that behave this way, it can be women as well. And it doesn't have to be, I mean a lad generally refers to a young male, it doesn't have to be a young male, it can also be a child or it could be an adult and so it's quite a broad term. And it's quite possibly derogatory towards males in some respects just by the naming it as lad culture.
>
> (Lydia, woman, U5)

> At the NUS [National Union of Students] conference there was an argument actually during a session, because other welfare officers thought that lad culture was just penalising men and actually it should be called lad and ladette culture. It should have a different name because what it is isn't about men's behaviour as a group, which is I think what everyone thinks of straight away, but it's about an attitude that we all have, which I thought was interesting.
>
> (Alex, woman, U4)

Such defensiveness from some women on behalf of men is neither surprising or new, and most likely reflects discourses about women as caring, and as carers and caretakers of men. Christina Hughes (2002, 72) highlights the dominance of the 'women are caring' discourse, arguing that women are positioned through the discourse of care:

> The good woman, like the good mother, is caring. ... She puts others before herself. ... Caring is seen to be an essential part of a woman's subjectivity. Thus, if a woman fails to care, if she fails to put others before herself, if she fails to take responsibility for others' needs, if she fails to show compassion, she is not a woman at all.

(Re)theorising and Addressing Lad Culture   113

As Jackson (2002, 44) has argued based on her work in secondary schools:

> girls are accustomed to their roles as supporters of the boys, and whilst many girls often regard boys as nuisances or pests, many girls do seem concerned that boys should not suffer as a result of initiatives introduced by the school, even if the girls feel that they themselves benefit from such initiatives.

Foster (1998) argues that this sort of caretaking is a fundamental expectation of women within education. She proposes that girls are the caretakers of males and of masculinity, and that they act to support the maintenance of male primacy and privilege in education. Thus, as Kenway and Willis (1998) observe, 'when boys complain that they are victims of EO [equal opportunities initiatives], it is the girls who most feel the effects, who suffer and rescue' (p. 151). This seems equally applicable to our higher education contexts.

The notion that 'it's not about men, it's an attitude we all have' epitomises the gender-blind discourse we are critiquing here and that was common in our research: 'I'm thinking of behaviour and instances here when I would want to apply a lad culture term and I wouldn't necessarily want to solely apply it to males' (Pete, man, U2). This broad conceptualisation of lad culture, which could include anyone, typically included harsh critiques of laddish women. As we saw in Chapter 3, women were judged disproportionately harshly relative to men for laddish behaviours. We argue that this stems from gender norms and expectations that, ironically, are rendered invisible in the gender-blind analyses of the majority of our interviewees.

As we discussed in Chapter 3, there were generally seen to be quantitative (more men are laddish and more often, and men perform more forms of laddism) and qualitative (men are more extreme) differences between men's and women's performances of laddism. Interviewees' attempts to offer a gender-neutral or gender-blind analysis often meant the women were judged disproportionately severely. For example, we noted that women's laddishness was defined almost entirely in relation to their heavy drinking, and occasionally linked to sport; they were not seen to perform the most pernicious aspects of lad culture such as sexism, racism, homophobia, sexual harassment, and violence. Nevertheless, despite this recognition they were judged relatively more harshly than laddish men. This parallels findings in Jackson's (2006b) work in secondary schools, where she found the same pattern from school staff about their perceptions of laddism among boys and girls. Jackson (2006b, 351–352) argued:

> Questions about whether and in what ways 'laddish' boys and girls differ prompted an interesting array of responses from teachers. Some teachers quantified the differences: 'I think laddish girls are

114 *(Re)theorising and Addressing Lad Culture*

not as laddish as boys' (Ms Stone, 3). Another suggested that boys are more 'laddish' because 'laddish boys have got a head start on these girls' (Ms Attwood, 3). However, despite the view that lads are more 'laddish' than 'ladettes', a number of the teachers suggested that 'laddish' girls were more difficult to deal with than 'laddish' boys (see also Younger *et al.*, 1999) and/or 'laddish' boys were more charming than their female counterparts.

Despite the quantitative and qualitative differences delineated by teachers in relation to laddish girls and boys – which mirror those narrated by staff in our higher education sample – laddish boys were portrayed as loveable rogues in ways that the girls never were. Jackson (2006b) explains this difference in relation to gender norms and expectations. She suggests that laddism among boys, while regarded by teachers as difficult and annoying in some situations, constitutes a conformity to gender norms and so is expected and often essentialised – 'boys will be boys'. Laddism among girls, on the other hand, represents a transgression of gender norms, and therefore incites severe condemnation (see also Jackson and Tinkler, 2007). Thus, the ostensibly 'gender-blind' approach and narratives about laddism espoused by staff in both the current research and Jackson's previous research are actually riven with gender norms and gender double-standards.

Thus, overall, an understanding of gender as a system of social organisation, as a binary social division, and as a set of socially and culturally determined expectations for men's and women's behaviour was absent from these discourses about who is laddish, and why they are laddish. Even when sexism, misogyny, and homophobia were named as key aspects of lad culture, they were very rarely named as linked to gender norms for men. Thus, masculinity as a concept, as a performance, was mentioned only by a few individuals. This suggests that sexism and harassment might be understood more clearly in terms of their effects, their impacts on women in particular, but are less readily understood in terms of their root causes. A limited understanding of underlying causes necessarily narrows the theorisation of factors that explain, perpetuate, and sustain lad culture.

'They Shouted at Her That They Wanted to Pin Her down and Rape Her': Lad Culture as Extreme and Visible

> Interviewer: … physical or sexual assault you wouldn't see as being part of the lad culture?
> I would see that as being just a really bad male.
>
> (Rebecca, woman, U4)

Lad culture was also characterised in terms of highly visible and 'extreme' behaviours or views. These were narrated as being infrequent and as perpetrated by problematic individuals: a few 'bad apples' or 'really bad males', in Rebecca's words. In conceptualisations of lad culture as extreme, rare, and deviant, examples primarily revolved around 'serious' sexism, sexual harassment, and/or sexual violence, for example, posting degrading, sexually objectifying memes on social media platforms, sexist and abusive chanting at women in public spaces, and sexual harassment and assault by individuals. In these narratives, the theorisation of specific incidents of harassment or abuse as particularly dangerous or perverse obscures the wider societal and cultural context in which such views and practices originate and are reproduced. The men who were identified as perpetrators of these acts were similarly viewed as unusually dangerous or problematic; and the ways in which their behaviours were linked to wider gender norms were rarely made visible in these narratives.

> The course team were concerned about his behaviour. But he would approach a student in the street and his own words at the end of a 15 second conversation he asked the student to go back to his room and have sex with him. He grabbed a female student round the throat and that's where the police were involved. He got, another student was very very drunk at one of the welcome parties in the halls and he was trying to forcibly take her back to his room. And so I think because he was, his behaviour was such that he was so blatant about what he was doing, that it was really quite easy for the halls to say that this is not acceptable and take the action they took as soon as the police arrested him.
>
> (Pete, man, U2)

> Well, we've had, you know, we have had a couple of sexual assaults on campus. But they have been, these are individuals who have mental health issues, they're not part of the rugby club or, you know, they're particular issues that we're trying to deal with. They've got mental health issues and so on. I haven't had any sexual assault reports by [meaning about] students who have not had a mental health issue.
>
> (Pat, woman, U2)

While we do not deny that some perpetrators of sexual violence have mental health issues, portraying perpetrators in this narrow and limited way is far from an accurate representation. As we have argued elsewhere:

> These are not acts committed by 'sex pests' or 'monsters'; these are not behaviours which are limited to certain environments. These behaviours reflect a wider culture in which sexual harassment and violence become normalised and routinized, in which the trivialisation and minimisation of such behaviours render them invisible and unspeakable.
>
> (Sundaram and Jackson, 2018, 4)

116   *(Re)theorising and Addressing Lad Culture*

While we take issue with the narratives of our interviewees, we understand why they have such perceptions: they reflect dominant discourses in UK society. Indeed, as we have noted, there were many parallels between the ways our interviews described laddism and the way it has been conceptualised and presented in the media. For example, laddism has been presented in the UK press largely in relation to students' social lives and most staff focused on this sphere, at least initially. Furthermore, reports about lad culture in the media have highlighted 'extreme' manifestations of laddish behaviour that are more likely to cause moral outrage. We recognise that there are plenty of examples of 'extreme' laddism. However, representing lad culture only as 'extreme' in its expression of sexism and misogyny tends to go hand-in-hand with portraying it as rare and perpetrated only by a 'few bad apples' who are easily identifiable. Such portrayals tend to render invisible lad culture's entanglements with other sexist practices and with wider social and cultural norms for gender behaviour. They work to pathologise a small number of 'extreme lads' and render invisible the broader socio-political discourses that normalise sexism and harassment as part of everyday life. Thus, it is both concerning yet understandable that for many of our interviewees lad culture was portrayed as 'extreme' and perpetrated in isolated incidents by a handful of problematic individuals with personality problems, rather than as a pervasive culture that produces, reinforces, and normalises gender-based harassment and violence in a range of forms.

> I would say here no, I wouldn't say we have a problem with lad behaviour at all. I would say that we're probably quite lucky in the sense that a lot of the time you just get one or two who are quite problematic, and it's more personality rather than a group thing.
>
> (Rebecca, woman, U4)

In critiquing such portrayals, we are not intending to criticise our individual interviewees. Their views reflect broader, very entrenched dominant discourses. Our aim, therefore, is to deconstruct and shift these dominant discourses, not least because they have important implications for how lad culture could and should be addressed, which we discuss later in this chapter. Now, we discuss how we theorise lad culture.

How Should We Theorise Lad Culture?

> I think it's the kind of pack mentality of normalising and allowing sexism and misogyny and a rape culture.
>
> (Kate, woman, U6)

To understand lad culture we need to acknowledge the structural and systematic gender inequality that underpins it. We suggest that the links

(Re)theorising and Addressing Lad Culture   117

between the wider cultural context and individuals' practices may be conceptualised and understood in terms of a pyramid (the concept of a 'pyramid of aggression' has also been referred to in Baynard, Plante, and Moynihan's [2005] work on sexual violence prevention in universities). A culture of everyday sexism – including 'banter', gender stereotyping, sexist and/or homophobic language, and benevolent sexism – forms the foundation for practices such as sexual harassment, gender-based violence, and rape, as the pyramid peaks. This conceptualisation allows us to shift the understanding of sexual and physical violence perpetrated in universities from being about the isolated acts of individuals to acknowledging the wider culture which allows, produces, and reinforces such practices. It enables the naming of gender norms and expectations that sustain harassment and violence, and which are embedded and normalised well before students enter tertiary education (Sundaram, 2014). It also enables a more intersectional understanding of such practices as located in a cultural context in which multiple hierarchies interlink, multiple systems of oppression co-exist, and sexist, racist, homophobic, disablist practices therefore cannot be conceived of as occurring in isolation.

The pyramid analogy can also be extended to understand the location of universities as contexts for sexual violence. Universities themselves can be understood as microcosms of the wider societal and cultural context, rather than as 'special' or unique sites in relation to sexual violence. Kelly (2016) has developed the concept of *conducive contexts* for violence against women and girls in order to focus our attention on the social, economic, and political conditions that enable violence, rather than focusing on the individual (perpetrators and) survivors. She argues that such contexts can be characterised as 'spaces in which forms of gendered power and authority and matrices of domination are in play' (Kelly, 2016, np). Particular features of higher education – including the marketisation of higher education as Phipps (2018b) has noted – may foster an increasingly 'conducive context' for hierarchy, oppression, and discrimination more generally. Hierarchy and competition permeate higher education institutions from the roots up, including in relation to evaluating teaching and research performance, valuing or dismissing some people within the institution differently from others, and the structure of the institution itself. The perceived function of universities reflects a wider societal turn towards neoliberalism, conservatism, and renewed discourses of 'value for money'. Universities may no longer be seen to be in a 'golden age' in which academics (albeit a small elite of mainly white, middle-class men) were free to pursue their own goals, and universities provided radical spaces for critical thinking and embracing a counter-cultural ethos and habitus (Tight, 2010). Now, they more frequently mirror and reinforce the discourses and hierarchies embedded in the wider cultural and societal context (Sundaram, 2018;

118   (Re)theorising and Addressing Lad Culture

Phipps, 2018b). We do not uncritically conceive of universities as 'danger zones', of course. As Lewis, Marine, and Kenney (2018) have noted, universities can and do represent unique sites for feminist activism and resistance. Within university microcosms, however, gender norms have and continue to produce gendered power relations through the gendered distribution of power, labour, and emotion which create the cultural foundation for other forms of gender inequality (Leathwood and Read, 2009). These include sexist language, banter, gender stereotyping, and sexual harassment and violence. So, universities can be understood as reflective of wider society, as well as embodying additional factors which we can theorise as perpetuating an individualised analysis of inequality, rather than a structural understanding of how and why gendered power inequalities arise.

Institutional/staff understandings of lad culture similarly fit onto a continuum which can be conceived of in terms of a pyramid. Understandings of lad culture map onto a continuum from broadly conceived to very specifically understood, but also on a spectrum from obscured and invisibilised to highly visible and high-profile. Within a pyramid model, the pervasive mis-recognition and invisibilisation of sexual harassment constitute a fertile base, or context, for other manifestations of sexual violence to be trivialised and dismissed. The highly visible cases, thought of as 'extreme', form the peak of the pyramid and are figuratively and literally represented as the minority of cases. The pervasive sexual harassment and abuse that women (and some men) students report experiencing in higher education contexts are hidden, like the base of an iceberg submerged under water, with only the tip of the pyramid visible as the 'real' problem of sexual violence in universities.

This depiction of institutional understandings links closely, as we have discussed, to dominant media representations of sexual harassment and violence being perpetrated by a handful of 'monsters' within university settings (for example, Sundaram and Jackson, 2018). The perpetrators are viewed as extreme, as are their behaviours; the wider cultural context and the myriad of ways and spaces in which women experience sexual violence are not acknowledged or viewed as relevant. Our pyramid model for theorising sexual violence in higher education also enables us to understand how universities are conducive cultural contexts for a range of gender inequalities, including sexual harassment and violence. We now move to consider how Connell's (2005) concept of gender regime may aid this understanding.

Gender Regimes

Connell's (2005) concept of the gender regime enables us to understand the ways in which sexism operates and is reproduced through the structures of the institution, creating a conducive context for sexual

(Re)theorising and Addressing Lad Culture   119

harassment and abuse to take place. The gender regime refers to 'the patterning of gender relations' (Connell, 2005, 6) in a given institution, which is rooted in and reflects the gender order of a wider social and cultural context. Connell notes that within a broader institutional context, local gender regimes may exist, and which do not mirror exactly the regime of the organisation. This presents a valuable conceptual tool for theorising variations in practice within institutions, as well as for understanding the reproduction and perpetuation of gender inequality within organisations as a whole. The gender regime can be understood as encompassing four dimensions of gender patterning: (1) the gendered division of labour, (2) gendered relations of power, (3) the gendering of emotion and human relations, and (4) the way gender difference is conceptualised and practiced in different arenas (Connell, 2005, 7).

Gender relations in higher education institutions remain heavily biased in favour of a white, middle-class and (straight, cis) male status quo. For example, recent research highlights the continuing underrepresentation of women and Black and minority ethnic (BME) staff in positions of power (Bhopal, 2018). The distribution of power within university contexts is highly gendered, as is the division of labour. AdvanceHE (2018) data show that in the United Kingdom: 75% of professors are men; men make up the majority of senior managers (69%); there is an overall gender pay gap (in favour of men) – the median pay gap is 13.7 percentage points and the mean is 17.2. The vast majority of administrative and secretarial roles within universities are held by women (81%). The picture is much worse when we also consider ethnicity: 68% of professors are white men and 23% are white women; 8% of professors are BME men and just 2% BME women. Of senior managers, 66% are white men and 30% are white women. Only 1.4% of senior managers are BME women and 3.5% are BME men.

So, hierarchies exist that reinforce power inequalities between men and other genders, between Black, minority ethnic, and ethnic majority staff, between academic and professional support staff, between research and teaching staff, and so on. The patterning of power relations continues to disadvantage women who are working-class, minority ethnic, disabled, and LGBTQ+; gender is one in a range of intersecting disadvantages. In this way, we can conceive of universities as a conducive context for abuses of power to occur.

A minority of our interviewees pointed to these structural inequalities, particularly in relation to gender, as factors that support and reinforce lad culture.

> Interviewer: Do you think senior management in the University could do more to tackle these problematic cultures on campus?
>
> Yeah, definitely. I think they definitely should be looking at it. But, again, I think it comes down to lack of women in senior roles. I think

120 *(Re)theorising and Addressing Lad Culture*

that's a big, big problem. Because you just get this kind of one-sided, you get this kind of [senior] level within Higher Education where you're just getting one kind of view in a way. I know that sounds terrible - them and us - and I don't mean it in that way at all, that directly. But you know, if you can't have diversity in senior management then it's going to be quite difficult to have diversity within the student body, because it all filters down ... I think a greater balance in senior management roles would be the first step I'd say. For me that's the root of the problem, because I would hope that would then foster a greater awareness, which would filter down ... I think senior management of the University needs to really look at what student culture is like. It's a very them and us thing, which is always going to be a little bit like that between students and tutors, but I think we need to try and break down those kind of barriers.

(Ella, woman, U2)

In accord with Ella's argument, we have seen how the gendered distribution of power within universities interacts with understandings of sexual violence, notions of visibility, veracity, and severity, to silence and invisibilise survivors' experiences. As noted in Chapter 4, university staff recognise some forms of harassment and violence and explicitly condemn these, while other manifestations of gender-based abuse are read less seriously, as being about 'boys having fun', 'drunkenness', or 'silliness'. The pervasiveness of everyday harassment in verbal, visual, physical, and sexualised forms comprise the fertile context – the base of the pyramid – in which more visible manifestations of sexual harassment and abuse can occur. Those university staff who might be responsible for responding to complaints or for enacting disciplinary processes are less likely to have everyday harassment and abuse made visible to them: 'I wouldn't say I see it a lot and I suppose over the time I've been doing the job you do get the odd case where a student says she's been raped' (Tracy, woman, U4). This combination of particular gendered power relations, the frequent lack of formal policies or processes for disclosing harassment and violence, and the minimisation or dismissal of everyday harassment by university staff can render universities *conducive contexts* for sexual harassment and violence.

Benefits of Adopting a Gendered Power Analysis of Lad Culture

The argument we are making here is not that student culture in the United Kingdom is distinctively conducive to lad culture; we are sceptical of the argument that lad culture is related to students, specifically. A gendered power analysis is fundamental for understanding how gender-based harassment and abuse arises and is sustained in university

(Re)theorising and Addressing Lad Culture   121

contexts. The pyramid model proposed in this chapter can incorporate intersecting identities, including ethnicity, social class, dis/ability, and sexuality, to understand how the cultural foundations for oppression and discrimination are laid through structure, representation, discourse, and individual practices. Universities are thus characterised by multiple, cross-cutting hierarchies that produce, sustain, and invisibilise many elements of lad culture.

There are persuasive reasons for adopting a gendered analysis of violence perpetration and of lad culture more broadly; we know that most of the sexist language, harassment, and abuse that is associated with lad culture is perpetrated by (cis, straight, white) men. Our data suggest that the majority of our participants recognise sexism to form the basis of lad culture, and rightly perceive this to be perpetrated primarily by men against women (Towl and Walker, 2019). Adopting a nuanced approach to understanding the ways in which gender, class, ethnicity, sexuality, and dis/ability (to name some characteristics) interact in experiences of harassment and abuse does not undermine a gendered analysis of these practices. Some women do exercise relative power over some men; racism and classism can be performed by women as well as men. However, it is the linkage to 'masculine' spaces, activities, and performances that demands an analysis of the practices associated with lad culture as gendered. These practices derive from what might be termed a 'masculinist ethics', a foregrounding of competition, power, and hierarchy. Feminist scholars across disciplines have theorised the ways in which 'masculinism' or a masculinist approach denotes an epistemology that is characterised by positivism, 'distance, disinterest, and disembodiment' (Sundberg, 2003, 188); an emphasis on individual rights rather than with collectivism or the systems that enable rights (Wicks, Gilbert and Freeman, 1994); and as transactional (Machold, Ahmed and Farquhar, 2007). This epistemological frame is useful for understanding how universities characterised by an increasingly competitive, individualised, and transactional ethos might foster a masculinist ethics and ethos. While we certainly do not advocate an essentialist lens or naturalised association of masculinity or masculinism with 'male' bodies, we do accept that gender norms and heteronormativity, in particular, align gender expectations with particular bodies (Paechter, 2006, 2012). We recognise the ways in which performances of lad culture, in the range of ways discussed in this book thus far, represent the institutionalisation and recirculation of gender norms.

Examples of lad culture that do not explicitly involve sexual harassment or violence, such as sports chanting, heavy and competitive drinking, and commandeering public spaces through disruptive behaviour are all practices that are reflective of gender norms and can therefore be conceptualised as 'gender-based'. Theorising lad culture more specifically as behaviour that reflects masculinist ethics or normative expectations

122 (Re)theorising and Addressing Lad Culture

for masculinity thus allows us to 'see' practices that may otherwise be essentialised, dismissed as being (gender neutral) 'student culture', trivialised as being about 'boys having fun', or as being about students managing transitions into higher education (as discussed in Chapter 4). A gendered analysis is therefore necessary for understanding the causes, manifestations, and impacts of practices associated with lad culture. However, a theorisation of the ways in which systems of power and hierarchy intersect also illustrates the need for an intersectional analysis of sexual harassment and violence in universities, and elsewhere. As Phipps reminds us:

> Of course, there is a need to preserve a focus on the binary gender hierarchy which continues to structure experience and discourse and which is underlined and maintained by sexist and harassing performances of laddism. However, while acknowledging that violence is still overwhelmingly perpetrated by men against women and people read as women, understanding why this occurs and how it relates to different expressions of masculinity requires more nuanced study.
>
> (Phipps, 2017a, 825)

The necessity of this nuanced analysis is crucial. In our study a prime example of this related to the intersection of gender and social class. Laddism in social spaces was very strongly associated with middle- and upper-class, straight, cis men and may be theorised particularly in relation to entitlement and masculinity. The laddism in teaching/learning spaces was different, however. While the sexist, misogynist behaviour of white men in elite settings may be read in relation to masculinity, white privilege, and entitlement, the disruptive behaviour in non-elite settings requires different consideration. In the case of the latter, while we also recognised the role of gender norms and masculinity, our analysis was attuned to the ways in which academia can alienate working-class students, and some laddish behaviours may reflect this. Thus, we must be careful, as Phipps (2017a) suggests, to theorise laddism differently according to the forms it takes and who is performing it. We argue that a gendered analysis is crucial to any theorisation of all forms of laddism, but other intersectional lenses are also essential to apply. How lad culture is theorised has implications for how it is addressed, or not, and it is to this that we now turn.

Addressing Lad Culture

How lad culture is theorised has important implications for how it is addressed both in and beyond universities. If causality is attributed to individuals' (or groups') behaviours rather than to a system of inequality, then a reactive and atomised approach to tackling the practices

(Re)theorising and Addressing Lad Culture   123

considered to be problematic will most likely be taken. If gender, power, and control are not recognised as linked to lad culture, then this will shape people's views on the practices that are considered to be problematic in the first place. Our analysis shows how specific elements of lad culture, such as sexual harassment, are not often seen as connected to wider practices involving abuses of power. The wider cultural context that underpins, produces, and sustains these aspects of lad culture is not understood or made visible in people's narratives; thus, interlinkages between different systems of oppression and discrimination are invisibilised. Intersections between gender, ethnicity, class, and sexuality in the perpetration, and experiences, of lad culture are invisibilised and can then be treated as separate, unconnected individual experiences. This is evident in the infrastructure and frameworks that universities have in place to deal with harassment. The 'structures and rationalities of the neoliberal university' (Phipps et al., 2018, 5) do not treat sexual harassment, racism, disablism, and homophobia and transphobia as (existing or) intersecting in one individual's (or group's) lived experience. Despite increasing emphasis by Universities UK (UUK) and the Office for Students to recognise hate crime on the basis of race/ethnicity and faith as an aspect of violence against women, few universities structurally enable challenge or prevention, let alone adequate support for survivors. So how is lad culture being addressed?

What Are Universities Doing to Address Lad Culture?

In our research most of the work to tackle lad culture was being undertaken, or at least driven, by the Student Unions rather than by the universities themselves. Indeed, this was a common pattern across the sector at the time. Such work, across the sector, typically included consent workshops; awareness raising campaigns; zero tolerance policies; clarifying complaints processes; banning initiation ceremonies; alcohol-free events in Freshers' week; highlighting experiences of sexual harassment through social media (for example Facebook pages) among others. Our interviews gave us insights not only into what initiatives were being implemented, but also some of the resistance and challenges faced by those who were leading them. For example, at University 4 the Student Union Equality Officer – Alex – had established a zero tolerance of sexual harassment policy within the Student Union venue on campus. The university was clearly supportive of this policy, and many of our interviewees pointed to it as the major way in which lad culture was being tackled. However, Alex's narrative was far less celebratory, as she recounted how difficult she had found it to implement.

> The policy was passed no problem, it's been making it procedure for the security staff here that's been the hurdle ... part of it is the

124 *(Re)theorising and Addressing Lad Culture*

> attitude of the security staff ... they do take their role really seriously and also the power that comes with that about being able to kick people out. And yet they are nervous to kick out someone who might be lying [being lied about] about harassment. They'll always point out that two or three years ago a girl said that a guy harassed her and it turned out that he hadn't and that [he] was her ex-boyfriend. But, yet they're really reluctant to err on the side of, well it should be a safe space anyway.

She conveyed how difficult it was to get the security staff to undertake the training, which she was left alone to provide because her male colleagues in the Student Union said they supported the policy but would not contribute in any way:

> But they've [the male security staff] been quite tight knit and difficult. I've been trying to get in touch with them all year actually. They have small staff meetings and so on and I never get invited at the right time or they tell me last minute and my calendar's full. So I think there's a bit of reluctance. So the training so far, yeah, it's just me and that's partly what I'm worried about because when I go, because this is the last time I can be around thankfully [laughs], there needs to be, this needs to be a collective responsibility, not just me.

Alex's narrative is revealing of the physical and emotional labour involved in starting up and developing such initiatives; such 'behind the scenes' accounts are rendered invisible when universities proudly point to their policies on sexual harassment. Indeed, the toll taken on student activists by such labour in this sphere is frequently invisible (Page, Bull and Chapman, 2019). Furthermore, Alex portrays the fragility of the scheme, both while it is in place (the security guards are reluctant to enact it) and longer term when it relies on the commitment and dedication of one person who has a short-term sabbatical post (as many Student Union staff do). Thus, while work to challenge lad culture must involve students and the Student Union, it must also be supported, 'owned', and sustained by universities. This view was espoused by many of our interviewees: 'I think it's not just Student Unions that are expected to tackle it; it's got to be institutions as well ideally in conjunction with students' (Chloe, woman, U6). Developing a collaborative and long-term strategy is also one of the five principles to tackle lad culture set out in the Tackling Lad Culture Benchmarking Tool (NUS, 2016).

More recently, there are hints that some universities are now doing more to tackle lad culture, largely because of the work of the UUK Task Force (2016, 2017, 2018) and £4.4 million funding incentive linked to that (Page, Bull and Chapman, 2019). As we discussed in Chapter 1, the UUK Task Force was established in autumn 2015 – around the time we

(Re)theorising and Addressing Lad Culture   125

finished our fieldwork – to examine violence against women, harassment, and hate crime in higher education, with a focus on students. The Taskforce made a number of recommendations for tackling these issues (UUK, 2016, 58–59) which we summarise here.

- Senior Leadership – all university leaders should afford tackling violence against women, harassment, and hate crime priority status and should dedicate appropriate resources to tackling it.
- Institution-wide approach – universities should take an institution-wide approach; provide progress reports and impact assessments to governing bodies; involve the Student Union in all elements.
- Prevention – universities should adopt an evidence-based Bystander Intervention Programme; highlight the behaviours that are expected from all students; set out disciplinary sanctions; embed a zero-tolerance approach; engage with local bars and nightclubs, student inductions, and student information; embed into human resources processes measures to ensure staff understand, and take responsibility for fostering, a zero-tolerance culture.
- Response – universities should develop a disclosure response for incidents of sexual violence and rape, work with external agencies and specialist services; take steps to implement a centralised reporting system; provide staff training.

We welcome the work of the group and the attention to violence against women, harassment, and hate crime. It has at least begun to acknowledge the issues, started a conversation, and prompted some universities to take some action, which many staff in our study called for:

> Well, I think if there could be some acknowledgement of the issue, that would be a great start. I think if you could get some institutions together and go, hey look there's this research, it says that it's an issue, we think it's an issue on our campuses too or in our university too, let's start a discussion. It's really simple, obviously, but I think if you could within the Higher Education sector get a few people and institutions to start doing that, that would be a massive leap forward just because I think it would empower many other people to acknowledge it. I would go so far as to say a zero tolerance on university property for this kind of culture and behavior.
>
> (Jessica, woman, U2)

However, as we noted in Chapter 1, both the report and recommendations missed the opportunity to highlight and address the fundamental role that gender norms and expectations play in producing and sustaining gender-based harassment and violence. While, of course, the recommendations do not preclude such a focus, the lack of such emphasis is

126 (Re)theorising and Addressing Lad Culture

disappointing, and is also reflected in the vast majority of the initiatives that were funded through this work and are reported as a series of case studies (UUK, 2017). We repeat that the work being done is, in general, to be welcomed, but the vast majority of it fails to acknowledge and address the structural gender inequalities (and other intersecting inequalities) that we argue are at the base of lad culture and gender-related violence. Drawing on Page, Bull, and Chapman's (2019) concept of 'slow activism', perhaps many, but certainly not all, of the recent spate of university-driven initiatives might be seen as quick fixes. While there is an urgent need to address lad culture, the danger of quick fixes, as Page et al. (2019, 1317) point out, is that 'Once a solution is put in place, regardless of its appropriateness and capacity to address the problem, it becomes very difficult to modify or change it'.

There is a danger of this occurring in the United Kingdom at the moment, where there is a substantial emphasis on bystander intervention training, largely because it was recommended by the UUK Task Force (2016). While we acknowledge that, if done well, Bystander Intervention Initiatives can bring benefits, they may be limited for addressing lad culture in several ways. First, while there is the *potential* for them to develop in-depth understandings among participants that lad culture is underpinned by gendered cultures, norms, and practices, they often do not. This may be because of time constraints – some programmes are delivered in as little as two hours (Bovill, 2019) – and because designers tend to draw mainly on psychological theories relating to social norms and bystander intervention when constructing the programmes. Perhaps the best known programme in the United Kingdom is one developed by Fenton, Mott, and Rumney in 2015, which is available for use free of charge (https://socialsciences.exeter.ac.uk/research/intervention initiative/). In their Theoretical Rationale for the initiative on the website, they emphasise that 'The educational programme delivered in this toolkit is underpinned by the theories of bystander intervention and social norms'. However, they do also add that 'Tackling domestic abuse and sexual coercion requires an appreciation that they are forms of behaviour which are rooted in gender relations and the social policing of gender roles in our society', and there is discussion of this in some sessions of the programme, which we very much welcome. Although Fenton, Mott, and Rumney offer an Intervention Toolkit that has eight sessions, our discussions with colleagues suggest that most adopt a much shorter version of the training, largely due to institutional or organisational constraints. As noted earlier, some are run over only two hours (Bovill, 2019). In such cases, discussion of the gender norms and inequalities that underpin lad culture, sexism, sexual harassment, and violence would be extremely limited or non-existent, as the focus is primarily on potential responses to such practices. Bystander Intervention Programmes also frequently fail to explore fully how intervention is

(Re)theorising and Addressing Lad Culture   127

much more risky for some than others, and these risks are shaped by structural and cultural inequalities such as gender, ethnicity, age, sexuality, dis/ability, and so on. A recent report by Page, Sundaram, Phipps, and Shannon (2019) contributes to our understanding of vulnerable or marginalised positionings from which intervention in sexual harassment and/or violence can be dangerous. They argue that 'bystander intervention [should be framed] as a mode of violence prevention, which is not uniformly available to all persons due to shared vulnerability characteristics' (p. 2). They offer institutional guidance regarding the ways in which different models of intervention, including staff disclosure training and bystander intervention, could incorporate a more explicit focus on power and privilege; the notion that a potential bystander might share vulnerability with a victim in terms of certain characteristics; and more diverse representations of perpetrators and victims in scenarios used in training (Page et al., 2019, 17). Thus, while we welcome well-designed and well-delivered intervention programmes that devote considerable time to engaging in depth with the ways that structural inequalities operate, they must not be the only initiatives employed.

Many of the strategies that are quickest and easiest to implement focus on individuals and many concentrate on disciplinary processes. We argue strongly that perpetrators need to be held to account, and that policies and practices for reporting and responding appropriately to sexual harassment and violence must be in place. However, we note Phipps' point that: 'When universities do take action, it is usually in an individualistic and punitive fashion which both fails to address the root problems and has tremendous potential to exacerbate additional inequalities' (Phipps, 2018a, 177). Some categories of people, notably those with less power, are likely to be punished more severely than others. We saw in Chapter 3, for example, how privileged students were more likely to be treated leniently because they 'knew how to play the game' and charmed their way out of trouble:

> they're well dressed, they come from a good background, they've managed to charm their way out of it, their father's a lawyer, they've maybe got a scholarship, they went to a good school, it's oh they've made a mistake, we'll move on.
>
> (Rebecca, woman, U4)

There were numerous accounts of the ways in which middle and upper-class white, heterosexual men would use their privilege to avoid sanctions:

> Their daddy would pay for it. So when it went wrong and the punt had sunk with people on board, daddy would take care of it or daddy's lawyer would take care of it.
>
> (Ruth, woman, U1)

128 *(Re)theorising and Addressing Lad Culture*

> But I think the fact that we will discipline people even if they get off in the end, has had a good effect on people. It's made people think, the college doesn't approve of this and I will be in trouble. Even if I end up having to tell my parents what's happened and they'll pay for a lawyer and they'll get me off it, it will nonetheless be a headache sort of thing.
>
> (William, man, U4)

Of course, not everyone has a lawyer on hand to 'get them off'. Thus, like Phipps (2018a), we argue that universities need to tackle the root causes. This is necessary not only because penal systems can reinforce inequalities, but also because they simply cannot work to challenge lad culture effectively. As we have seen, it is pervasive and normalised, these factors, along with many others – shame, lack of trust in the systems, fear – mean that the vast majority goes unreported. Thus, systems of individual punishment are inadequate. We need broader, systemic change, alongside some of the step changes we are already witnessing.

Such systemic cultural change will be neither easy nor quick. However, there are examples of institutions – notably the University of Sussex and Imperial College London – that have commissioned the Changing University Cultures Collective (CHUCL) to undertake in-depth research on institutional culture, driven in large part by what might be referred to as lad culture (https://chucl.com/). Furthermore, there are also some good examples of work that has provided training for university staff who may be dealing with students' disclosures of sexual violence that are premised on understanding the relationship between sexual violence and cultural norms and gender inequality (Alldred and Phipps, 2018). Such work is essential, as flagged in our research:

> there is definitely a need to improve that system, the training that goes with that, the personal tutors. I think not just in relation to the laddism culture but just sort of welfare in general. Personal tutors don't always seem to be particularly able to deal with difficult issues.
>
> (Tracy, woman, U4)

This is the type of work – slow activism – that we need in universities if we are to address the roots of lad culture.

Even with slow activism we need to be careful to evaluate the impacts across a range of social categories. We discussed earlier, for example, the need to challenge current gender regimes in higher education, which is essential. We referred in that section to inequalities between university staff, and noted the ways in which the distribution of power within university contexts is highly gendered. There are initiatives in place to attempt to address this, most notably Athena Swan. Athena Swan is a

(Re)theorising and Addressing Lad Culture   129

charter of what was the Equality Challenge Unit and now is AdvanceHE. It recognises good practice towards the advancement of gender equality and although there are numerous important and valid criticisms of it, it has promoted gender equality in several ways. However, the benefits are not shared equally among all groups of women, with the main beneficiaries being white, middle-class women (Bhopal, 2019). While there is also a Race Equality Charter, Bhopal and Henderson (2019) argue based on their research of both Charters (Race Equality and Athena Swan) that in higher education policy-making there has been a privileging of gender over race in terms of addressing inequalities in higher education. Thus, in implementing strategies we need to be mindful of intersecting inequalities, and monitor the effects carefully.

Our final point here is that addressing the roots of lad culture, sexual harassment, and gender-related violence should be on the agenda long before university. As the work of Sundaram (2014) and others has shown, and as Jessica (U2) eloquently conveys, tackling sexual harassment and violence in a preventative way through deconstructing gender norms and structures should begin in primary school:

> You know, it comes back to the basic ideas around equality actually. And that we still live in a society … where we don't have proper full relationships with sex education in schools. Because that's what it really comes down to: if you equip young people from the off, from age 5, to say we're all equal, this is how we talk about relationships and negotiate, and this is how we do these things. I mean to me, that's the only way we'll actually begin to really challenge it.
>
> (Jessica, woman, U2)

Summary

In this chapter we argued for a (re)theorisation of lad culture that takes into account the hegemony of binary gender relations, the multiple and intersecting ways in which gender is performed, and the role of gendered organisational regimes of higher education institutions in fostering particular values. We argued that the maintenance of binary gender relations is key to the perpetuation of lad culture; however, such features and mechanisms are habitually concealed by dominant gender-blind analyses. Thus, we presented a reconceptualisation of lad culture that makes visible the gendered norms and expectations that underpin it, and takes into account the ways these intersect with other structural inequalities in specific contexts. We finished the chapter by arguing that attempts to tackle lad culture will only be successful if they understand and target the root causes of it and that, unfortunately, currently too few initiatives do this.

Note

1 We are not suggesting that sexual violence is generally highly visible. We know that most sexual violence is hidden and not reported. What we are referring to here are cases that become highly visible because they have been witnessed or reported. Their high visibility relates to their 'extremeness' and their perceived (rather than actual) rarity.

Conclusion

> I suppose it's [lad culture] one of those concepts that's slightly elastic isn't it, it includes lots of different things. And so it's useful as a means of exploring something, but it may be that as you're starting to become more analytic that you have to start maybe categorising things in a more thematic way. Because the concept itself could include so many different things, it lacks that kind of explanatory power in the end.
>
> (Diana, woman, U4)

Diana's insightful thoughts exemplify many of the issues that we have been grappling with throughout this book as we have explored the questions: what is lad culture, where is it evident, who is laddish, and how can we explain and theorise it? The concept of lad culture is, as Diana suggests, elastic: it is flexible, stretchy, and expandable. While the vast majority of our participants identified similar core features of lad culture, beyond those the concept was restricted or stretched in various different ways. This elasticity is crucial to acknowledge and understand: we have argued that how lad culture is conceptualised affects perceptions about its pervasiveness, location, who performs it, how it may be explained, and how it should be addressed. So interviewees' answers to the question what is lad culture shape their responses to the where, who, and why questions. Importantly, we argue that dominant current conceptualisations about lad culture render less visible its pervasiveness, who is laddish, and the causes of laddism.

Where Is Lad Culture?: The In/Visibility of Lad Culture Itself

As we saw in Chapter 2, current dominant discourses about laddism render lad culture itself less visible in and to higher education institutions in four main ways. First, despite staff acknowledging that sexism and sexual harassment and violence are central to lad culture, dominant discourses associating lad culture with alcohol-fuelled public displays of rowdiness mean that many of the less extreme 'everyday' instances of sexual harassment and violence across a wide range of university contexts

132　*Conclusion*

are rendered invisible. Second, and closely related, only high-profile, extreme cases received staff attention and action. Third, the association of lad culture with social spaces and alcohol led to a common perception among staff that lad culture was not visible to them because they did not frequent spaces in which laddish practices occurred. This association compartmentalised and limited it, meaning that, initially at least, staff were less likely to 'see' lad culture in teaching/learning spaces. However, once participants moved away from a one-dimensional understanding of lad culture, they 'saw' and named numerous examples of this culture in teaching/learning, support, and departmental contexts. Fourth, the normalisation of lad culture rendered it less visible. The ubiquity of sexual harassment was, ironically, one of the reasons it is not highlighted or reported. It was seen to be almost nowhere because it was everywhere. It was so commonplace that it was normalised. Thus, its ubiquity and normalisation contributed to its invisibility: it was not made visible to higher education institutions by students through complaints processes. Thus, overall, dominant discourses about the nature of lad culture serve to reduce its perceived prevalence.

Who Is Laddish?: The In/Visibility of White, Upper- and Middle-class, Heterosexual Men

In Chapter 3 we argued that lad culture within our higher education institutions was most associated with middle- and upper-class, white-UK, young, heterosexual, cis men. In some ways, then, this group was rendered visible in lad culture discourses across these sites. However, at the same time, other discourses about laddism served to render them less visible. As we explored in the last chapter, laddism was often dichotomised and conceptualised as very broad *and* as visible and extreme. When conceptualised as visible and extreme, laddism was narrated as being performed by a very small number of unusual and dangerous men – a few bad apples or 'monsters' – who were frequently positioned as having personality problems and/or mental health issues. By contrast, the broad conceptualisation of lad culture meant that anyone (of any gender) could be laddish. Thus, in these conceptualisations, white, middle- and upper-class, heterosexual men lose their centrality and visibility.

Why Is There Laddism?: The In/Visibility of Gender Norms and Expectations

In Chapter 4 we saw that staff narrated explanations for men's laddism in a variety of ways. The vast majority lacked any gendered analysis and instead referred to peer group influences and the need to fit in, (in)authenticity, banter, age/maturity, effects of alcohol, and/or the freedom afforded by a university context. Those who mentioned gender either tended to essentialise laddism as 'boys being boys' or, conversely, suggest

Conclusion 133

that 'it's only banter, they don't really mean it'. While contradictory, both types of explanations served to discursively reduce men's accountability. The dominance of these gender-blind explanations served to render invisible the gender norms, expectations, and structural intersecting inequalities that underpin and sustain lad culture.

The Combined Effect

Overall, dominant discourses about lad culture in higher education institutions underestimate the prevalence and frequency of laddism in these contexts, making visible only the most extreme examples. Although on the one hand middle- and upper-class, white, heterosexual, cis men are identified as the group most associated with lad culture in higher education, on the other hand the focus on this elite group is substantially blurred and thus obscured. It is obscured by conceptualisations of lad culture that identify a few unusual, rare, dangerous men as the real concern, or by notions that anyone can be laddish, lad culture is not tied to particular groups, and, indeed, it is unfair to tie it to men only. This gender-blind approach dominated explanations for laddism, and thus served to largely remove men and masculinities from the analysis.

Lad culture was most often understood as a 'problem of individuals', rather than as located in wider social and gendered norms. This narrative serves to diffuse the problem, viewing it as one perpetrated by a few, problematic men, thus undermining its pervasiveness as well as the individual and collective impact on survivors of living and working within university contexts that are conducive to such practices. The notion of a 'pack mentality', which is often associated with lad culture, was associated with *individual* groups and sub-cultures within university settings, not seen as linked to wider cultural, social, political norms, or contexts. This focus on individuals and specific groups (e.g. sports teams) obscures the extent and impact of laddism, as well as its causes.

We argue that to challenge lad culture we first have to make visible the scale of the problem. Given that current conceptualisations mask the scale, we need to find ways of understanding lad culture that render it visible. We have offered such a framework in Chapter 5, one based on an analysis of gender, power, and other intersecting inequalities. Yet, given the ways that conceptualisations of lad culture currently seem to minimise and trivialise it, and also locate the problem as belonging to multiple groups all at once, it is pertinent to ask whether the concept of lad culture has value: should we be attempting to shift the conceptual terrain?

The Term 'Lad Culture'

The term *lad culture* is culturally and historically diffused and difficult to pin down. For example, Phipps and Young (2015b) show

134   *Conclusion*

how the term "laddish" was used in the 1950s to define readers of magazines like Playboy; it is also reminiscent of the working class "new lad" constructs of the 1990s. In relation to class, our student participants in the larger study had difficulty defining "the lad," sometimes associating him with cigarettes, beer cans, and hoodies, and other times with rugby shirts and the financial capacity to drink and socialize, both falling on opposite ends of cultural stereotypes of class. Lad culture is also globally slippery. For example, in Silvia's previous educational experience in Spain, the term *lad culture* did not exist, while behaviors that could be defined as laddish did. Concurrently, British lad culture shares much with the American "frat boy" culture. These issues raise a number of questions beyond the scope of this article, but include the naming of "lad culture" as a useful device to mobilize feminist action, but also concerns that in naming it, we risk deeming invisible both historical and global instances of sexism, misogyny, and violence against women in contexts where such terminology do not exist.

(Diaz-Fernandez and Evans, 2019b, 245)

Diaz-Fernandez and Evans succinctly and precisely summarise several thorny issues associated with the term 'lad culture' and echo many of our own concerns and tensions with the term, which have been highlighted and discussed at various points throughout this book.

The looseness of the term and its shifting meanings, applications, and associations were discussed in the Introduction to this book and also in Chapter 1. We noted that lad culture was applied in secondary schools in the 1990s and early 2000s in ways that share some similarities with, but also important differences from, the way it has been applied in higher education contexts over the last decade. In schools, lad culture was most closely associated with 'uncool to work' discourses that are almost entirely absent in higher education (Jackson, 2006; Jackson and Dempster, 2009). Similarly, as we noted in the Introduction, and as Diaz-Fernandez and Evans observe, the social class associations have shifted considerably. Many of our interviewees also discussed this. Such shifting meanings and associations combined with the general nebulousness of the term lead to confusion. Jackson's (2006a, 2006b, 2010a) work in secondary schools showed that, much like our study here, there were seen to be core aspects of lad culture that most pupils and teachers had shared understandings of, but there were also some important differences. As Jackson argued, teachers who were tasked by the Government with challenging lad culture did not share a common understanding of what they were meant to be tackling. In some cases this led to considerable confusion and problematic practices as we explored earlier in this book (Jackson, 2010a). Our study has revealed a remarkably similar pattern. Thus, a lack of shared understanding about lad culture is a significant

Conclusion 135

problem, especially if those tasked with challenging it do not have clear ideas about what it is they are challenging.

There are also numerous other problems. As Catherine Nixey writing in *The Times* (19/03/2013) argues, the term lad culture may mask the more problematic elements of it, suggesting that 'laddism' is a 'jolly term' for what is 'sexual harassment'. This was a view shared by many of our interviewees:

> I think it kind of glamourizes it calling it lad culture I have to say. I think it should just be called sexual harassment, because that is a much uglier word. You know, lad culture is sort of like, oh yeah, you know, we're all one of the lads and everything. And it bigs it up a bit and I think it shouldn't. I think it should be called something else which isn't quite as glamorous and describes it how it is.
>
> (Pat, woman, U2)

Indeed, one interviewee suggested that it might be seen as a badge of honour: 'The labelling thing has given those who've done it a slight sense of pride: well it's all right to behave like this, I've just been lad-dish' (William, man, U4). A small minority of our interviewees did see lad culture as largely unproblematic, and many more highlighted what they saw to be the positive aspects of it, for example, male bonding and 'having a laugh'. Relatedly, as we have argued, its association for many people primarily with alcohol, sports and social activities and spaces compartmentalises and limits it, and in some cases can be used to (uncritically) explain or even excuse it:

> and a possible cause is actually ... the camaraderie in these large groups of boisterous males and the camaraderie that that's the done thing, and they enjoy spending time with these guys and behaving in the way they do and having a few too many drinks and saying some things they probably shouldn't. It's a culture of, they might actually think it's quite fun to do these things. And the culture they're a part of, they enjoy being a part of.
>
> (Jim, man, U4)

The UK-specific nature of the term, as Diaz-Fernandez and Evans (2019) articulate, makes international dialogue much more difficult, what they refer to as lad culture being 'globally slippery'. As we have seen, although lad culture is a UK-specific term, the behaviours and attitudes associated with it are certainly not UK-specific. However, the specific term renders the sexism, misogyny, sexual harassment, and violence that it entails less visible as a global phenomenon.

There are some *potential* advantages to the term. The notion of 'culture' is important. As Phipps and Young note (NUS, 2013, 13) the notion

136 *Conclusion*

of culture is complex but approximates to a set of shared values, attitudes beliefs, and behaviours among a particular group. Thus, the notion of a culture should avoid reproducing the myth that sexual harassment and violence are conducted by individual 'monsters' in an otherwise utopia of equality. However, as we have seen, in practice this myth was still apparent and strong, despite the inclusion of the term 'culture'.

The breadth of the concept lad culture has both advantages and disadvantages; we have discussed this in some depth. The potentially positive aspect relates to the breadth of a continuum of laddism. This enables us to link sexist comments and 'jokes' and physical assault, thus highlighting the ways in which seemingly 'trivial' comments and behaviour scaffold sexual assault and contribute to a culture in which women (and various other groups) are cast as less worthy. However, as we discussed, the tendency to dichotomise laddism – into very broad and extreme – generally obfuscates this relationship. Furthermore, the breadth is used to suggest that anyone of any gender can be laddish, thus obscuring the gendered underpinnings of lad culture and precluding a gendered analysis.

Overall, the term is problematic in a host of ways, and even its potential advantages seem to get lost in translation as it moves from academic into popular discourse. Nevertheless, it is a term that currently has a lot of traction and is unlikely to disappear anytime soon. Thus, we must continue to problematise the term when we engage with it, and attempt to foster understandings and theorisations of it that make visible lad culture's entanglements with social and cultural norms for gender behaviour, as well as other structural social inequalities. Only then will we be able to devise effective strategies to challenge it, and such challenges are essential: 'It's fundamentally about equality and as long as we have such a dominant lad culture, we're not going to have equality and we can't expect to' (Jessica, woman, U2).

Appendix
Interview Schedule

Background

- What's your role?
- Number of years in the role.
- Previous roles at this institution.
- Time at this institution.
- Time and roles at previous institutions.

1. What do you understand by the term 'lad culture'?
2. Do you think lad culture is evident in higher education?
3. Is lad culture evident at this university?
4. Is lad culture more evident in some contexts than others?
5. Is laddism more likely to be performed by some individuals or groups than others?
6. Is lad culture new (or re-emerging)?
7. What do you think motivates laddism?
8. Are lad cultures problematic?
9. Is laddism evident among university staff?
10. Is the university doing anything to tackle lad cultures?
11. Do you know of any initiatives at any other higher education institutions to tackle lad culture?
12. Does more need to be done to tackle lad cultures in higher education and, if so, what?

References

Abrahams, J. (2017). "Honourable mobility or shameless entitlement? Habitus and graduate employment." *British Journal of Sociology of Education* **38**(5): 625–640.

AdvanceHE (2018). Equality + higher education: Staff statistical report 2018.

Ahmed, S. (2010). *The promise of happiness*. Durham, NC, Duke University Press.

Ahmed, S. (2017). *Living a feminist life*. Durham, NC, Duke University Press.

Alldred, P. and A. E. Phipps, Eds. (2018). *Training to respond to sexual violence at European universities: Final Report of the USVreact Project*. Middlesex, Brunel University London Press.

Anderson, E. (2010). *Inclusive masculinity: The changing nature of masculinities*. London, Routledge.

Anderson, E., M. McCormack and H. Lee (2012). "Male team sport hazing initiations in a culture of decreasing homohysteria." *Journal of Adolescent Research* **27**(4): 427–448.

Archer, L. (2006). Masculinities, femininities and resistance to participation in post-compulsory education. In C. Leathwood and B. Francis (eds) *Gender and lifelong learning: Critical feminist engagements*. London, Routledge: 70–82.

Armstrong, E. A., L. Hamilton and B. Sweeney (2006). "Sexual assault on campus: A multilevel, integrative approach to party rape." *Social Problems* **53**(4): 483–499.

Australian Human Rights Commission (2017). *Change the course: National report on sexual assault and sexual harassment at Australian universities*. Sydney, Australian Human Rights Commission.

Bailey, L., C. Griffin and A. Shankar (2015). "'Not a good look': Impossible dilemmas for young women negotiating the culture of intoxication in the United Kingdom." *Substance Use and Misuse* **50**(6): 747–758.

Banyard, V. L., M. M. Moynihan and E. G. Plante (2007). "Sexual violence prevention through bystander education: An experimental evaluation." *Journal of Community Psychology* **35**(4): 463–481.

Banyard, V. L., E. G. Plante and M. M. Moynihan (2005). *Rape prevention through bystander education: Bringing a broader community perspective to sexual violence prevention*. Washington, DC, U.S. Department of Justice.

Bathmaker, A.-M., N. Ingram, J. Abrahams, A. Hoare, R. Waller and H. Bradley (2016). *Higher education, social class and social mobility: The degree generation*. London, Palgrave Macmillan.

140   References

Berkowitz, A. D. (2004). The social norms approach: Theory, research, and annotated bibliography. http://alanberkowitz.com/articles/social_norms.pdf

Bhopal, K. (2018). *White privilege: The myth of a post-racial society*. Bristol, Policy Press.

Bhopal, K. and H. Henderson (2019). "Competing inequalities: Gender versus race in higher education institutions in the UK." *Educational Review*: 1–17.

Bordo, S. (2004). *Unbearable weight: Feminism, Western culture, and the body*. Oakland, University of California Press.

Bourdieu, P. (1984). *Distinction: A social critique of judgement of taste*. London, Routledge.

Bovill, H. (2019). Report of research exploring first-year undergraduates' awareness, confidence to intervene, and intervention behaviours with regard to sexual and domestic abuse on campus and evaluation of an optional 2 hour bystander programme. Bristol, University of West of England.

Brook (2019). Sexual violence and harassment in UK universities. http://legacy.brook.org.uk/data/Brook_DigIN_summary_report2.pdf

Brownmiller, S. (1975). *Against our will: Men, women and rape*. New York, Simon and Schuster.

Bull, A. and R. Rye (2018). *Silencing students: Institutional responses to staff sexual misconduct in higher education*. Portsmouth, The 1752 Group/University of Portsmouth.

Burke, P. J., G. Crozier, B. Read, J. Hall, J. Peat and B. Francis (2013). *Formations of gender and higher education pedagogies (GaP)*. York, Higher Education Academy.

Campbell, S. (1994). "Being dismissed: The politics of emotional expression." *Hypatia* 9(3): 46–65.

Cantor, D., B. Fisher, S. H. Chibnall, R. Townsend, H. Lee, G. Thomas, C. Bruce and I. Westat (2015). *Report on the AAU campus climate survey on sexual assault and sexual misconduct*. Washington, DC, Association of American Universities

Cheeseman, M. J. (2010). The pleasures of being a student at the University of Sheffield. PhD, University of Sheffield.

Clare, J. (2003). Respect for teacher 'is key to boys doing well' Ofsted study finds bad teaching can promote a laddish culture. *The Daily Telegraph*: 5.

Clarke, V. (2018). "'Some University Lecturers Wear Gay Pride T-shirts. Get Over It!': Denials of homophobia and the reproduction of heteronormativity in responses to a gay-themed t-shirt." *Journal of Homosexuality*: 1–25.

Coker, D. (2018). "Restorative responses to campus sexual harm: Promising practices and challenges." *The International Journal of Restorative Justice* 1: 385–398.

Collins, E. (2016). "The Criminalisation of Title IX." *Ohio State Journal of Criminal Law*, 13(2): 365–395.

Collins, T. (2009). *A social history of English Rugby Union*. London, Routledge.

Connell, R. (2005). *Masculinities*. Cambridge, Polity.

Copenhaver, S. and E. Grauerholz (1991). "Sexual victimization among sorority women: Exploring the link between sexual violence and institutional practices." *Sex Roles* 24(1): 31–41.

DeGue, S., L. A. Valle, M. K. Holt, G. M. Massetti, J. L. Matjasko and A. T. Tharp (2014). "A systematic review of primary prevention strategies for sexual violence perpetration." *Aggression and Violent Behavior* 19(4): 346–362.

References   141

DeKeseredy, W. and K. Kelly (1993). "The incidence and prevalence of woman abuse in Canadian University and college dating relationships." *The Canadian Journal of Sociology/Cahiers canadiens de sociologie* 18(2): 137–159.

DeKeseredy, W. S. and M. D. Schwartz (1997). *Woman abuse on campus: Results from the Canadian National Survey.* London, Sage.

DeKeseredy, W. S., M. D. Schwartz and S. Alvi (2000). "The role of profeminist men in dealing with woman abuse on the Canadian College campus." *Violence against Women* 6(9): 918–935.

Dempster, S. (2007). Degrees of laddishness: Masculinities within the student experience of higher education. PhD, Lancaster University, UK.

Dempster, S. (2009). "Having the balls, having it all? Sport and constructions of undergraduate laddishness." *Gender and Education* 21(5): 481–500.

Dempster, S. (2011). "I drink, therefore I'm man: Gender discourses, alcohol and the construction of British undergraduate masculinities." *Gender and Education* 23(5): 635–653.

Department for Education and Employment (2000). "Boys must improve at same rate as girls – Blunkett." 2006, www.dfee.gov.uk/pns/DisplayPN.cgi?pn_id=2000_0368

Department of Education (2018). "Secretary DeVos: Proposed Title IX Rule Provides Clarity for Schools, Support for Survivors, and Due Process Rights for All." 30/09/2019 www.ed.gov/news/press-releases/secretary-devos-proposed-title-ix-rule-provides-clarity-schools-support-survivors-and-due-process-rights-all

De Visser, R. O. and J. A. Smith (2007). "Alcohol consumption and masculine identity among young men." *Psychology and Health* 22(5): 595–614.

Diaz-Fernandez, S. and A. Evans (2019a). "Lad culture as a sticky atmosphere: Navigating sexism and misogyny in the UK's student-centred nighttime economy." *Gender, Place & Culture*: 1–21.

Diaz-Fernandez, S. and A. Evans (2019b). "'Fuck Off to the Tampon Bible': Misrecognition and researcher intimacy in an online mapping of 'Lad Culture'." *Qualitative Inquiry* 25(3): 237–247.

Drinkaware (2015). Drinkaware drunken nights out student harassment survey – summary. www.drinkaware.co.uk/research/our-research-and-evaluation-reports/dno-student-harassment-survey-summary/

Edley, N. and M. Wetherell (1997). "Jockeying for position: The construction of masculine identities." *Discourse and Society* 8(2): 203–217.

Epstein, D., J. Elwood, V. Hey and J. Maw, Eds. (1998). *Failing boys? Issues in gender and education.* Buckingham, Open University Press.

Fisher, B., F. T. Cullen and M. G. Turner (2000). *The sexual victimization of college women.* Washington, DC, US Department of Justice.

Ford, K. A. (2011). "Doing fake masculinity, being real men: Present and future constructions of self among Black college men." *Symbolic Interaction* 34(1): 38–62.

Foster, V. (1998). Education: A site of desire and threat for Australian girls. In A. Mackinnon, I. Elgqvist-Saltzman and A. Prentice (eds) *Education into the 21st Century: Dangerous terrain for women?* London, Falmer Press: 81–93.

Francis, B. (1999). "Lads, Lasses and (New) Labour: 14–16-year-old students' responses to the 'laddish behaviour and boys' underachievement' debate." *British Journal of Sociology of Education* 20(3): 355–371.

142 *References*

Francis, B. and L. Archer (2005). "Negotiating the Dichotomy of Boffin and Triad: British-Chinese pupils' constructions of 'laddism'." *The Sociological Review* 53(3): 495–521.

Francis, B., C. Skelton and B. Read (2010). "The simultaneous production of educational achievement and popularity: How do some pupils accomplish it?" *British Educational Research Journal* 36(2): 317–340.

Francis, B., C. Skelton and B. Read (2012). *The identities and practices of high achieving pupils: Negotiating achievement and peer cultures.* London, Bloomsbury Publishing.

Frintner, M. P. and L. Rubinson (1993). "Acquaintance rape: The influence of alcohol, fraternity membership, and sports team membership." *Journal of Sex Education and Therapy* 19(4): 272–284.

Frosh, S., A. Phoenix and R. Pattman (2001). *Young masculinities: Understanding boys in contemporary society.* Basingstoke, Palgrave.

García-Favaro, L. and R. Gill (2016). "'Emasculation nation has arrived': Sexism rearticulated in online responses to Lose the Lads' Mags campaign." *Feminist Media Studies* 16(3): 379–397.

Gill, R. (2003). "Power and the production of subjects: A genealogy of the new man and the new lad." *The Sociological Review* 51(1_suppl): 34–56.

Gill, R. (2016). "Post-postfeminism?: New feminist visibilities in postfeminist times." *Feminist Media Studies* 16(4): 610–630.

Graham, K., I. Wilson and A. Taft (2017). "The broader context of preventing alcohol-related intimate partner violence." *Drug and Alcohol Review* 36(1): 10–12.

Harnett, R., B. Thom, R. Herring and M. Kelly (2000). "Alcohol in transition: Towards a model of young men's drinking styles." *Journal of Youth Studies* 3(1): 61–77.

Harris, A. (2004). *Future Girl: Young women in the twenty-first century.* London, Routledge.

Hearn, J. (2004). "From hegemonic masculinity to the hegemony of men." *Feminist Theory* 5(1): 49–72.

HM Government (2012). *Call to end violence against women and girls.* London, HM Government.

HM Government (2019). *Ending violence against women and girls, 2016–2020, strategy refresh.* London, HM Government.

Hughes, C. (2002). *Women's contemporary lives: Within and beyond the mirror.* London, Routledge.

Jackson, C. (2002). "Can single-sex classes in co-educational schools enhance the learning experiences of girls and/or boys? An exploration of pupils' perceptions." *British Educational Research Journal* 28(1): 37–48.

Jackson, C. (2003). "Motives for 'laddishness' at school: Fear of failure and fear of the 'feminine'." *British Educational Research Journal* 29(4): 583–598.

Jackson, C. (2006a). *Lads and ladettes in school: Gender and a fear of failure.* Maidenhead, Open University Press.

Jackson, C. (2006b). "'Wild' girls? An exploration of 'ladette' cultures in secondary schools." *Gender and Education* 18(4): 339–360.

Jackson, C. (2010a). "'I've been sort of laddish with them … one of the gang': Teachers' perceptions of 'laddish' boys and how to deal with them." *Gender and Education* 22(5): 505–519.

References 143

Jackson, C. (2010b). "Fear in education." *Educational Review* 62(1): 39–52.

Jackson, C. and S. Dempster (2009). "'I sat back on my computer ... with a bottle of whisky next to me': Constructing 'cool' masculinity through 'effortless' achievement in secondary and higher education." *Journal of Gender Studies* 18(4): 341–356.

Jackson, C., S. Dempster and L. Pollard (2015). "'They just don't seem to really care, they just think it's cool to sit there and talk': Laddism in university teaching-learning contexts." *Educational Review* 67(3): 300–314.

Jackson, C., C. Paechter and E. Renold, Eds. (2010). *Girls and education 3–16: Continuing concerns, new agendas*. Maidenhead, Open University Press.

Jackson, C. and N. Sherriff (2013). "A qualitative approach to intergroup relations: Exploring the applicability of the social identity approach to 'messy' school contexts." *Qualitative Research in Psychology* 10(3): 259–273.

Jackson, C. and V. Sundaram (2018). "'I have a sense that it's probably quite bad ... but because I don't see it, I don't know': Staff perspectives on 'lad culture' in higher education." *Gender and Education*: 1–16.

Jackson, C. and P. Tinkler (2007). "'Ladettes' and 'modern girls': 'Troublesome' young femininities." *The Sociological Review* 55(2): 251–272.

Jeffords, S. (1994). *Hard bodies: Hollywood masculinity in the Reagan era*. New Brunswick, Rutgers University Press.

Jeffries, M. (2019). "'Is it okay to go out on the pull without it being nasty?': Lads' performance of lad culture." *Gender and Education*: 1–18.

Jensen, M.B. and G. Hunt (2019). "Young women's narratives on sex in the context of heavy alcohol use: Friendships, gender norms and the sociality of consent." *International Journal of Drug Policy*: 1–8.

Kehily, M. J. and A. Nayak (1997). "'Lads and laughter': Humour and the production of heterosexual hierarchies." *Gender and Education* 9(1): 69–88.

Kelly, L. (2016). "The conducive context of violence against women and girls." *Discover Society*. https://discoversociety.org/2016/03/01/theorising-violence-against-women-and-girls/

Kenway, J. and S. Willis (1998). *Answering back: Girls, boys and feminism in schools*. London, Routledge.

Kimmel, M. (2008). *Guyland: The perilous world where boys become men*. London, Harper.

Koss, M. P., C. A. Gidycz and N. Wisniewski (1987). "The scope of rape: Incidence and prevalence of sexual aggression and victimization in a national sample of higher education students." *Journal of Consulting and Clinical Psychology* 55(2): 162–170.

Koss, M. P. and C. J. Oros (1982). "Sexual experiences survey: A research instrument investigating sexual aggression and victimization." *Journal of Consulting and Clinical Psychology* 50(3): 455–457.

Krebs, C. P., C. H. Lindquist, T. D. Warner, B. S. Fisher and S. L. Martin (2007). The Campus Sexual Assault (CSA) Study: Final Report. www.ncjrs. gov/pdffiles1/nij/grants/221153.pdf

Leathwood, C. (2013). "Re/presenting intellectual subjectivity: Gender and visual imagery in the field of higher education." *Gender and Education* 25(2): 133–154.

Leathwood, C. and B. Read (2008). Gender and the Changing Face of Higher Education: A Feminized Future?, Society for Research into Higher Education/ Open University Press.

144 *References*

Lebreton, F., R. L. Peralta, J. Allen-Collinson, L. C. Wiley and G. Routier (2017). "Contextualizing students' alcohol use perceptions and practices within French culture: An analysis of gender and drinking among sport science college students." *Sex Roles* 76(3–4): 218–235.

Lewis, R., S. Marine and K. Kenney (2018). "I get together with my friends and try to change it. Young feminist students resist 'laddism', 'rape culture' and 'everyday sexism'." *Journal of Gender Studies* 27(1): 56–72.

Light, R. and D. Kirk (2000). "High school rugby, the body and the reproduction of hegemonic masculinity." *Sport, Education and Society* 5(2): 163–176.

Loh, C., C. A. Gidycz, T. R. Lobo and R. Luthra (2005). "A prospective analysis of sexual assault perpetration: Risk factors related to perpetrator characteristics." *Journal of Interpersonal Violence* 20(10): 1325–1348.

Lund, E. M. and K. B. Thomas (2015). "Necessary but not sufficient: Sexual assault information on college and university websites." *Psychology of Women Quarterly* 39(4): 530–538.

Machold, S., P. K. Ahmed and S.S Farquhar (2007). "Corporate Governance and Ethics: A Feminist Perspective." *Journal of Business Ethics* 81(3): 665–678.

MacNell, L., A. Driscoll and A. N. Hunt (2015). "What's in a name: Exposing gender bias in student ratings of teaching." *Innovative Higher Education* 40(4): 291–303.

Marine, S. B. and Z. Nicolazzo (2017). "Campus sexual violence prevention educators' use of gender in their work: A critical exploration." *Journal of Interpersonal Violence*: 1–23.

Marsh, H. (2018). The student drinking experience: Expectations, friendship and drinking practices. PhD, Lancaster University, UK.

Martin, P. Y. and R. A. Hummer (1989). "Fraternities and rape on campus." *Gender & Society* 3(4): 457–473.

Mazar, L. A. and A. Kirkner (2016). "Fraternities and campus sexual violence: Risk, protection, and prevention." *Violence and Gender* 3(3): 132–138.

McCarry, M. (2010). "Becoming a 'proper man': Young people's attitudes about interpersonal violence and perceptions of gender." *Gender and Education* 22(1): 17–30.

McCormack, M. (2012). *The declining significance of homophobia.* Oxford, Oxford University Press.

Mills, M. (2001). *Challenging violence in schools.* Buckingham, Open University Press.

Mitchell, K. M. W. and J. Martin (2018). "Gender Bias in Student Evaluations." *PS: Political Science & Politics* 51(3): 648–652.

Nicholls, E. (2019). *Negotiating femininities in the neoliberal night-time economy: Too much of a girl?* Cham, Springer International Publishing.

Nichols, K. (2018). "Moving beyond ideas of laddism: Conceptualising 'mischievous masculinities' as a new way of understanding everyday sexism and gender relations." *Journal of Gender Studies* 27(1): 73–85.

NUS (2010). *Hidden Marks: A study of women students' experiences of harassment, stalking, violence and sexual assault.* London, NUS.

NUS (2013). *That's what she said: Women students' experiences of 'lad culture' in higher education.* London, NUS.

NUS (2014). *Lad culture and sexism survey: August-September 2014.* London, NUS.

References 145

NUS (2016). *Tackling lad culture benchmarking tool*. London, NUS.

NUS (2018). *Power in the academy: Staff sexual misconduct in UK higher education*. London, NUS.

Nyström, A.-S., C. Jackson and M. Salminen Karlsson (2019). "What counts as success? Constructions of achievement in prestigious higher education programmes." *Research Papers in Education* 34(4): 465–482.

O'Connor, E. C., T. E. Ford and N. C. Banos (2017). "Restoring threatened masculinity: The appeal of sexist and anti-gay humor." *Sex Roles* 77(9): 567–580.

Paechter, C. (2006). "Reconceptualizing the gendered body: Learning and constructing masculinities and femininities in school." *Gender and Education* 18(2): 121–135.

Paechter, C. (2012). "Bodies, identities and performances: Reconfiguring the language of gender and schooling." *Gender and Education* 24(2): 229–241.

Page, T., A. Bull and E. Chapman (2019). "Making power visible: 'Slow Activism' to address staff sexual misconduct in higher education." *Violence against Women* 25(11): 1309–1330.

Page, T., V. Sundaram, A. Phipps and E. Shannon (2019). Developing an Intersectional Approach to Training on Sexual Harassment, Violence and Hate Crimes: Guide for Training Facilitators. York.

Pedersen, W., H. Copes and S. Sandberg (2016). "Alcohol and violence in nightlife and party settings: A qualitative study." *Drug and Alcohol Review* 35(5): 557–563.

Phipps, A. (2017a). "(Re) theorising laddish masculinities in higher education." *Gender and Education* 29(7): 815–830.

Phipps, A. (2017b). "Speaking up for what's right: Politics, markets and violence in higher education." *Feminist Theory* 18(3): 357–361.

Phipps, A. (2018a). 'Lad culture' and sexual violence against students. In N. Lombard (ed) *The Routledge handbook of gender and violence*. London, Routledge: 171–182.

Phipps, A. (2018b). "Reckoning up: Sexual harassment and violence in the neoliberal university." *Gender and Education*: 1–17.

Phipps, A. and G. Smith (2012). "Violence against women students in the UK: Time to take action." *Gender and Education* 24(4): 357–373.

Phipps, A., J. Ringrose, E. Renold and C. Jackson (2018). "Rape culture, lad culture and everyday sexism: Researching, conceptualizing and politicizing new mediations of gender and sexual violence." *Journal of Gender Studies* 27(1): 1–8.

Phipps, A. and I. Young (2015a). "Neoliberalisation and 'lad cultures' in higher education." *Sociology* 49(2): 305–322.

Phipps, A. and I. Young (2015b). "'Lad culture' in higher education: Agency in the sexualization debates." *Sexualities* 18(4): 459–479.

Rawlings, V. (2019). "'It's not bullying', 'It's just a joke': Teacher and student discursive manoeuvres around gendered violence." *British Educational Research Journal* 45: 698–716.

Read, B., P. J. Burke and G. Crozier (2018). "'It is like school sometimes': Friendship and sociality on university campuses and patterns of social inequality." *Discourse: Studies in the Cultural Politics of Education*: 1–13.

Reay, D. (2017). *Miseducation: Inequality, education and the working classes*. Bristol, Policy Press.

146 References

Renold, E., S. Bragg, C. Jackson and J. Ringrose (2017). How gender matters to children and young people living in England. http://orca.cf.ac.uk/107599/1/How%20Gender%20Matters.pdf

Revolt Sexual Assault and The Student Room (2018). Students' experience of sexual violence. https://revoltsexualassault.com/wp-content/uploads/2018/03/Report-Sexual-Violence-at-University-Revolt-Sexual-Assault-The-Student-Room-March-2018.pdf

Richardson, D. and H. May (1999). "Deserving Victims? Sexual Status and the Social Construction of Violence." *The Sociological Review* 47(2): 308–331.

Ringrose, J. (2012). *Postfeminist Education?* London, Routledge.

Rivers, I. (2015). Homophobic and transphobic bullying in universities. In H. Cowie and C. A. Myers (eds) *Bullying among university students: Cross-national perspectives*. London, Routledge: 48–60.

Romero-Sánchez, M., V. Toro-García, M. A. H. Horvath and J. L. Megías (2017). "More than a magazine: Exploring the links between lads' mags, rape myth acceptance, and rape proclivity." *Journal of Interpersonal Violence* 32(4): 515–534.

Rose, G. (2001). *Visual methodologies*. London, Sage

Ryan, K. M. and J. Kanjorski (1998). "The Enjoyment of Sexist Humor, Rape Attitudes, and Relationship Aggression in College Students." *Sex Roles* 38(9): 743–756.

Sanday, P. R. (2007). *Fraternity gang rape: Sex, brotherhood and privilege on campus*. New York, New York University Press.

Seabrook, R. C., L. M. Ward and S. Giaccardi (2018). "Why is fraternity membership associated with sexual assault? Exploring the roles of conformity to masculine norms, pressure to uphold masculinity, and objectification of women." *Psychology of Men & Masculinity* 19(1): 3–13.

Sheard, L. (2011). "'Anything could have happened': Women, the night-time economy, alcohol and drink spiking." *Sociology* 45(4): 619–633.

Sherriff, N. (2007). "Peer group cultures and social identity: An integrated approach to understanding masculinities." *British Educational Research Journal* 33(3): 349–370.

Skeggs, B. (1997). *Formations of class and gender*. London, Sage.

Skeggs, B. (2001). "The toilet paper: Femininity, class and mis-recognition." *Women's Studies International Forum* 24(3): 295–307.

Skeggs, B. (2004). *Class, self, culture*. London, Routledge.

Skelton, A. (1993). "On becoming a male physical education teacher: The informal culture of students and the construction of hegemonic masculinity." *Gender and Education* 5(3): 289–303.

Stanko, E. A. (1990). *Everyday violence: How women and men experience sexual and physical danger*. New York, HarperCollins.

Stentiford, L. J. (2019). "'You can tell which ones are the laddy lads': Young women's accounts of the engineering classroom at a high-performing English university." *Journal of Gender Studies* 28(2): 218–230.

Sundaram, V. (2014). *Preventing youth violence: Rethinking the role of gender and schools*. London, Palgrave.

Sundaram, V. and C. Jackson (2018). "'Monstrous men' and 'sex scandals': The myth of exceptional deviance in sexual harassment and violence in education." *Palgrave Communications* 4(1): 147.

References 147

Sundberg, J. (2003). "Masculinist epistemologies and the politics of fieldwork in Latin Americanist geography." *The Professional Geographer* 55(2): 180–190.

Thomae, M. and A. Pina (2015). "Sexist humor and social identity: The role of sexist humor in men's in-group cohesion, sexual harassment, rape proclivity, and victim blame." *Humor* 28(2): 187–204.

Tight, M. (2010). "The golden age of academe: Myth or memory?" *British Journal of Educational Studies* 58(1): 105–116.

Towl, G. J. and T. Walker (2019). Tackling Sexual Violence at Universities: Themes and perspectives. In G. J. Towl and T. Walker (eds) *Tackling sexual violence at universities: An international perspective*. London, Routledge: 1–10.

Tyler, I. (2008). "Chav Mum Chav Scum." *Feminist Media Studies* 8(1): 17–34.

Universities UK (2016). Changing the Culture: Report of the Universities UK Taskforce examining violence against women, harassment and hate crime affecting university students. UUK, London.

Universities UK (2017). Changing the culture: Responding to cases of violence against women, harassment and hate crime affecting university students. Directory of case studies. UUK, London.

Universities UK (2018). Changing the culture one year on: An assessment of the strategies to tackle sexual misconduct, hate crime and harassment affecting university students. UUK, London.

Walker, R. and I. Goodson (1977). Humour in the classroom. In P. Woods and M. Hammersley (eds) *School experience. Explorations in the sociology of education*. London, Routledge: 196–227.

Warin, J. (2010). *Stories of self: Tracking children's identity and wellbeing through the school years*. Stoke-on-Trent, Trentham Books.

Warin, J. and S. Dempster (2007). "The salience of gender during the transition to higher education: Male students' accounts of performed and authentic identities." *British Educational Research Journal* 33(6): 887–903.

Wicks, A. C., D. R. Gilbert Jr and R. E. Freeman (1994). "A feminist reinterpretation of the stakeholder concept." *Business Ethics Quarterly:* 4(4): 475–497.

Willis, P. (1977). *Learning to Labour: How working class kids get working class jobs*. Farnborough, Saxon House.

Women and Equalities Committee (2016). *Sexual harassment and violence in schools*. London, Government Equalities Office.

Younger, M. and M. Warrington with R. McLellan (2005). *Raising boys' achievement in secondary schools: Issues, dilemmas and opportunities*. Maidenhead, Open University Press.

Index

academic achievement 4–7, 55–56, 69–70, 91, 100–105, 107
acceptance *see* fitting in
accountability 12, 28, 30–31, 72–74, 84, 133
addressing lad culture 21, 25–32, 57–59, 95–96, 122–129
AdvanceHE 119, 129
age 3–5, 15, 23–24, 48, 51, 54, 56, 64–68, 72–75, 78–84, 96–98, 100, 103, 112
Ahmed, Sara 49, 59
alcohol 3, 6–8, 16–17, 20, 22–23, 25–26, 35, 38, 40–45, 47–48, 54, 56–58, 62–69, 71–73, 76–78, 80, 85, 87–88, 91, 98–100, 111–113, 115, 121, 123, 131–132, 134–135
alienation 103–105
Archer, Louise 79–80, 105
Athena Swan 128–129
Australia 8, 14, 20, 23, 44, 83
authenticity 12, 86, 89–93, 98, 132

banter 1, 7, 12, 16–17, 33, 38, 45–54, 72, 83, 86, 88, 93–96, 111, 117–118, 132–133
bars, pubs and nightclubs 37–42, 48, 50, 54, 59, 71, 74, 99, 108, 111, 125
Blunkett, David 4
BME students and staff 45, 54, 71, 119
boys-will-be-boys discourse 12, 82, 96–98, 112–114
boys' 'underachievement' 2, 4–7, 69
bro culture 11, 14, 21–23, 32
Brook 17–18
Bullingdon Club 71, 84–85
Burkinshaw, Paula 53
bystander intervention 28–29, 125–127

Campus Sexual Assault survey 19
Canada 14, 19

care discourses 112–114
Centers for Disease Control and Prevention (CDC) 28
challenging lad culture *see* addressing lad culture
Changing University Cultures Collective (CHUCL) 27, 128
chanting 2, 36, 46–51, 65, 76–78, 87–88, 94–96, 111, 115, 121
Cheeseman, Matthew 50, 94–95
Chinese students and lecturers 79–81, 84, 103–104
Clery Act 27–28, 30
Collins, Tony 75–76
competition 4, 12, 22–25, 27, 86, 95, 106–108, 117, 121
complaints processes 27–28, 39, 49, 58–59, 120, 123, 128
Connell, Raewyn 24, 41, 119
continuum of laddism 16, 35, 75, 91, 96, 110, 118, 136
culture change 1, 21, 27–32, 123–129

DeVos, Betsy 28
Dempster, Steve iv, 15–16, 25, 35, 41, 64–65, 75, 81, 87–92, 105
Diaz-Fernandez, Silvia 38–41, 133–135
dis/ability 17, 25, 29, 30, 45, 48, 68, 117, 119, 121, 123, 127
disruptive students 4–7, 12, 51–52, 54–56, 66, 69–70, 84, 102–105, 111, 121–122
Drinkaware 17
drinking *see* alcohol
drugs 34, 98–99, 106

entitlement 12, 18, 72–78, 84, 106, 122
entitled immunity 12, 72–73, 84
essentialising laddism 12, 86, 96–100, 112, 132

150 Index

ethnicity 11–12, 30, 35, 45, 48, 61, 68, 78–81, 119–121, 123, 127–129
Evans, Adrienne 38–41, 133–135
Everyday Sexism Project 8, 40

fear 7, 16, 40, 45, 87, 89, 107, 128
fitting in 12, 65–66, 86–92, 94, 96, 107, 111, 132
football 3–4, 41, 48, 52–53, 71–72, 75, 89, 91, 94
Francis, Becky 5, 79–80
frat culture 8, 11, 14, 20–23, 26, 32, 42, 134
freshers' week 38, 43, 123

geek 1, 38, 91
gender-blind approaches 13, 68, 108–116, 129, 132–133
gender double-standards 6, 12, 62–69, 72, 84, 114
gender norms and expectations 12, 27, 29, 31, 108, 110–122, 125–129, 132–133
gender pay gap in higher education 119
gender regimes 118–120, 128
Gill, Rosalind 3, 90, 93
group behaviours 4–5, 7–8, 15, 17, 21–23, 35–36, 45, 47, 53, 66–67, 70, 74–79, 86–89, 91–92, 94–95, 111, 116, 132–133, 136
guy code 21, 92

hate crime 26, 123, 125
hazing see initiation rituals
hegemonic masculinity 24–25, 34, 41, 44–47, 57, 61, 64, 88–89
heterosexuality 20, 24–25, 46–48, 60, 88–89, 94, 106, 119, 121–122, 127, 132–133
Hidden Marks study 7, 16
homophobia 2, 7, 11, 16–17, 29, 33, 35, 37, 45–48, 50–51, 53, 67, 88, 94–96, 101, 111, 113–114, 117, 123
Hughes, Christina 112
humour see jokes

initiation rituals 1, 11, 23, 33, 42–45, 47, 76–78, 87, 112, 123
intergroup relations 80–81, 94
in/visibility of lad culture 8, 18, 34, 55–59, 76–78, 80–81, 130–133

Jackson, Carolyn x, 3–6, 21–22, 34, 53, 63–64, 80–81, 90, 102–103, 105, 107–108, 113–115, 134
Jeffries, Michael 88, 91, 94, 96
jokes 17, 35, 47–51, 54–55, 93–96, 107, 110–111, 136

Kimmel, Michael 21, 43

laddish staff 51–54, 83–84
laddish women see ladettes
ladettes 3, 6, 11–12, 62–69, 72, 84, 112–114
lectures see teaching/learning contexts

male bonding 16, 53, 112, 135
management/business schools 52, 55, 70, 83, 102–103
marketisation of higher education 45, 58, 95, 117
masculinist ethics 121
mature students 54, 56, 81–83
media reports 1–5, 7, 18, 34, 50–51, 57, 63–64, 72, 76, 81, 108–110, 116, 118, 135
#MeToo 1, 8, 81
mental health 18, 28, 115, 132
Miliband, David 4–5

National College Women Sexual Victimisation Survey 19
National Union of Students (NUS) 1, 7, 13, 16–18, 26, 112, 124
neoliberalism 40, 45, 58, 107–108, 117, 123
new lad 2–3, 90, 134
new man 3, 90
Nichols, Kitty 82
night-time economy see bars, pubs and nightclubs
Norway 99

online harassment see social media

pack mentality see group behaviours
Pederson, Willy 98–99
Phipps, Alison ix, x, 1–2, 7, 16–19, 35–36, 42, 45, 47–48, 55, 58, 61, 70, 81, 101, 107–109, 111, 122–123, 127–128, 133, 135–136
poor-boys discourse 92
post-1992 universities 9–10, 55–56, 70, 88, 94, 102

Index 151

power in the Academy study 18
pre-1992 universities 9–10, 55, 64, 70, 75, 87, 100–101
prevalence of lad culture 7, 14, 19–23, 49, 51, 55–59, 69–71, 81, 87, 92, 132–133; *see also* in/visibility of lad culture
privilege 12, 25, 31, 69–74, 76–79, 84–85, 92, 95–96, 106, 113, 122, 127–128, 132–133; *see also* entitlement
private schools 73, 76, 77–78
punishment 25–26, 72–74, 111–112, 127–128
pyramid model of lad culture 117–118, 120–121

racism x, 11, 33, 35, 46–47, 50, 59, 62, 67, 76–77, 91, 95, 101, 103–104, 111, 113, 121, 123
rape 19, 22, 28, 29, 36, 38, 57, 78, 96–97, 117, 125
rape culture 1, 17, 22, 29, 36–38, 78, 96–97, 114, 116–117
reporting 17–20, 26–28, 30, 39–41, 56–59, 68, 125–127; *see also* complaints processes
research methods 9–11, Appendix
Revolt Sexual Assault 17
rugby 1–2, 12, 36, 41–44, 50, 65, 74–78, 82, 84, 89, 91, 94, 108, 115, 134

secondary school 2–7, 15, 21–22, 28, 41, 44, 53–55, 61, 69–70, 73–74, 77–81, 84, 90, 102, 105, 107, 113–114, 127, 129, 134
security staff 8, 10, 41, 68, 79, 123–124
The 1752 group 18
sex and relationships education 129
sexual harassment policies 26–31, 120, 123–124, 127
slow activism 126, 128
social class 2, 4–5, 11–12, 15, 25, 30, 34, 45–48, 64–66, 69–79, 88–89, 102–103, 105, 117, 119, 121–123, 127–129, 132–134

social media 10, 36–37, 45, 54, 80–81, 108, 115, 123
sport 1, 4–5, 7, 16–17, 20, 22–23, 26–27, 34–35, 41–48, 50, 53, 62–66, 74–78, 83, 87, 106, 111–113, 121, 133, 135; *see also* football; rugby
sports science 52, 102–103
staffing profile of higher education 119
student feedback 55, 101–102
The Student Room 9, 17
Sundaram, Vanita 31, 34, 58, 115, 127, 129

Tackling Lad Culture Benchmarking Tool 124
teaching/learning spaces 20, 46, 51–56, 70–71, 84, 100–105, 122, 132
teaching/learning methods 58, 102–105
Title IX 27–28, 30
transition 38, 43, 88–90, 96, 107, 123; *see also* initiations
transphobia 29, 60, 123
trivialisation 12, 22, 31, 36, 49, 51, 54, 93, 96–100, 106, 115, 133

uncool-to-work discourses 4–7, 134
Universities UK (UUK) 26–29, 59, 123–126
university leadership 10, 53, 78, 119–120, 125
United States of America (US) 2, 8, 11, 14, 19–23, 27–32, 42, 134

visibility of lad culture *see* in/visibility of lad culture

Warin, Jo ix, 89, 92–93
widening participation 71
Willis, Paul 2, 5, 15, 69

Young, Isabel 1, 16–17, 36, 42, 45, 47–48, 107, 133, 135

zero tolerance policies 8, 26, 123–125